Carol Neal

EYES TO BEHOLD HIM

EYES TO BEHOLD HIM

MICHAEL J. GAYDOS

Creation House
Carol Stream, Illinois

Contents

Dedicated to the Christian Community, both Catholic and Protestant, who have loved me and accepted me into their hearts and homes, and to the many priests and ministers who have so graciously opened their pulpits to me.

Introduction

In December 1970, just before Christmas, I was sitting in a prayer and praise service at a church in Pittsburgh, Pennsylvania. As I sat in the service that Sunday evening, with Christians of all denominations lifting their hands and worshiping the Lord, I heard a voice in my spirit: "Michael, stand and announce the good news. Tell these people that if they will take off their glasses on Christmas Day, I will heal their eyes as I have healed yours. I will give them a Christmas gift that no one else can give, a Christmas gift that money cannot buy."

I was quite young in my experience with the Holy Spirit and I was unaccustomed to hearing the Lord speak to me in such a dramatic way. I later recalled reading J. B. Phillips' *Your God Is Too Small.** So often we limit what God can do because man is limited and we project our own limitations upon God. So I censored the message: "That's just not possible!"

* Macmillan, New York, 1960.

As the service continued, every word that was said and every song that was sung indicated that I should give this message. The more I sat there trying to resist it, the more the Spirit of God urged me to speak.

Finally, at the close of the meeting more than an hour later, the pastor called upon me for a closing prayer. I suddenly had the microphone in my hand. How could I avoid it any longer? The pastor was both surprised and delighted to hear the prophecy as I spoke in fear and hesitation.

During the Christmas holidays I visited in several homes which had been represented in that Sunday evening service. Glasses—on the tree, under the tree, by a manger scene—they made my Christmas so exciting! At least ten persons confirmed their healings to me. How many more were healed on Christmas Day I do not know. Most of the worshipers that Sunday evening wanted a healing, but only those who heard the word and received the word and acted upon the word received the fulfillment of the promise.

*   *   *   *   *   *

A surprising new word, "book," began appearing in my thoughts last spring. Other people mentioned the idea to me also. Occasionally someone would ask, "Why don't you write a book?" I could sense something developing but I thought, *This is nothing more than another ego trip.* Still the word "book" continued to occur to me.

I'll settle this once and for all, I decided. *Lord, you know I don't have writing skills. If you really want me to write a book, then you have a publisher approach me with a proposal. That should end it!* I thought.

The Greater Pittsburgh Charismatic Conference began with a talk by John Sherrill, Senior Editor of *Guideposts* and author of a number of books. He was a last-minute replacement for Maria von Trapp, who was unable to come as advertised. The Conference Committee had also asked the manager of Creation House to represent the Baroness at this session. Since Creation House was publishing her forthcoming autobiography, *Maria,* he had been asked to share briefly with the Conference some anecdotes from her life.

Rather than commute to and from home, I took a dormitory room at Pittsburgh Theological Seminary. I was locking the door of my room when I saw a familiar face. I recognized John Sherrill from his picture. He, too, was leaving the dormitory for the opening Clergy Banquet. I introduced myself. "John, I'm Mike Gaydos, a member of the Planning Committee. May I show you the way to the meeting?"

John was very gracious. We discussed his work for a few minutes and then he asked about my ministry. I told him briefly what God had been doing in my life for the past two years. John said, "Did you ever consider writing a book about your experiences?"

"Well, yes. But I thought it might just be another ego trip."

"Mike, if you do decide to write, and you think I can help, please contact me."

Was this an answer to my request? Was this God's go-ahead signal?

I felt it wasn't a clear indication. I'd much rather have fireworks, sirens, and flashing green lights.

After the Clergy Banquet we went upstairs into the sanctuary of the huge gothic East Liberty Presbyterian Church. It was already jammed. I found a seat across the chancel from the pulpit. The publisher's representative was seated behind the pulpit in preparation for his address. He was looking around at the awesome, overflowing crowd. When his eyes focused upon me, he instantly heard a voice in his spirit: *He has a book!*

Although he quickly looked away from me his curiosity was captured. Nonchalantly he looked around the congregation, his view sweeping slowly toward me again. As his gaze fell upon me—and I was utterly unaware of the little drama developing—a voice fairly shouted in his spirit: *Book!* Instead of looking away, he took careful note of my face and appearance, intending to talk to me after the service.

At the appointed time he rose to speak. Looking around at his audience and concentrating upon his subject, he inadvertently glanced at me again. *Book!* interrupted his thoughts and momentarily left him robbed of what he was planning to say. Interestingly enough, I hardly heard anything he said. I was lost in thoughts of my own, quietly weeping and sensing that God was trying to tell me something.

When the meeting ended, he made his way quickly toward my seat, but I had already moved out with the crowd. He searched frantically, but I was lost from his view amid the surging crowd of 2,500 persons. "Oh well," he sighed. "I guess there wasn't anything to it. I'll probably never see that priest again."

He returned to his dormitory room at the Pittsburgh Theological Seminary where most of the Conference was being held. Still pondering the strange message, he went to bed. The next morning he entered the men's room. There I was, brushing my teeth!

Excitedly he told me what had transpired. I became embarrassed instead of excited. The very thought of writing a book actually embarrassed me. I put him off by saying that I'd let him know. He must have felt rather deflated.

I could hardly sleep that night because of the flow of conflicting emotions within me. Perhaps God didn't provide fireworks, but He had made a rather convincing case for a book. Still not satisfied, I cautiously asked the advice of a number of clergymen whose judgment I respect— Michael Esses of Melodyland in Anaheim, California; George Stockhowe of St. Martin's Episcopal Church; Dick Goodhart of Eighth United Presbyterian Church; John Blewitt of Penn Hills Presbyterian Church; Russ Bixler of the Church of the Brethren, and several other charismatic leaders. Without exception all these men encouraged me to go ahead with the book. "God will use it to heal His people's eyes!" was a common observation.

Still I felt strangely embarrassed: *Perhaps this is merely what I suspected—a big ego trip.*

Sometimes I felt almost like an unwilling actor in an amateur play, the one actor who knows the least about what is going on. Finally my own mind began to catch up with what God was doing. It was not an easy decision to go ahead, because I knew that my ability to perceive God's leading was clouded by the mixed feelings of excitement, timidity, and wonder over the sovereignty of God in the matter. God had indeed sovereignly ordained this book. My problem was praying through self-consciousness, the utter embarrassment I felt at thinking of myself writing a book. The Lord has helped by telling me—through many other people—that this is *His* book, *His* business and *His* plans to bless *His* children by means of it.

So it has become a project filled with a mixture of painful memories and thrilling anticipation of the future. It is a story of a personal quest, a seeking for identity, fulfillment, significance, and especially love and affection. Pope John, that beloved, saintly man, wrote his autobiography, *Journal of a Soul.* I suppose each man who reaches out for God, desiring a deeper communion with Him, could entitle his own walk as the journal of a soul.

Each time I relate my testimony before a group—and now in writing it out—I relive "the agony and the ecstasy." It reopens old wounds, yet the Lord uses the retelling to heal others who have been similarly hurt! I have long since discovered the truth of the hymn writer's words, "What He's done for others He can do for you." As each reader sees these words, I pray that he will perceive that all God has done for me—and more—God will also do for the reader. Jesus Christ will save you, rescue you, redeem you, forgive your sins, wash you with His blood, fill you with His Spirit, and heal you in body, mind and spirit. Praise His holy name! Receive all that He wants to give you as you read this book.

So it was with the encouragement of Creation House and numerous friends that I left home on a dual mission —to continue my ministry of witnessing to the grace of the Lord Jesus Christ and to begin putting together in a continuous whole a written witness of that grace in my own life.

I look upon Father Michael Scanlan as my primary spiritual advisor. I feel also that I should voluntarily submit myself to other respected clergymen with spiritual maturity. In this regard I have also asked Dick Goodhart, John Blewitt, Russ Bixler, George Stockhowe, and Ralph Wilkerson to be my counselors. I talked with Father Scanlan and he reported that no bishop had yet agreed to sponsor me in the Seminary. Father Scanlan's guidance— and he prayed quite a bit about me—was that I should continue to give my witness for another year as the Lord leads. How I appreciate a seminary rector filled with the Holy Spirit! The direction of my work was confirmed by others.

Most amazing to me is that I, the neurotic worrier, was embarking upon this new project. Barely beneath the surface of my conscious thoughts was a growing anxiety about seminary. *Do I complete my schooling this year or not?* I wondered.

But I was determined that worrying was dead with the old Mike. This problem belonged to Jesus. I looked upon the lack of sponsorship for seminary as guidance: my future was still open. When July 1 passed, I began confirming speaking invitations beyond the end of summer. Without this freedom no book could have developed.

1

Rejection

When I was nine months old I contracted a very serious case of whooping cough. Subsequently I lost nearly all sight in the left eye and the vision was greatly impaired in the right eye. But far worse than the loss of sight were the intense academic, social, athletic, and psychological scars and traumas that resulted. At the age of one I began to wear glasses. The doctor put a patch over the right eye to try to force me to use the left eye. I also was required to visit the optometrist several times a week for treatments and eye exercises.

I recall attending first grade, sitting in crushing embarrassment, humiliation, and frustration over my inability to master reading skills because of the glasses and the patch. I was nearly blind when I wore the patch, yet until the doctor realized the obvious, I had to wear it. Consequently I failed the first grade.

Not only was I a failure in the classroom, but also on the playground. With no depth perception I couldn't meet the

ball with the bat. I was repeatedly humiliated by screaming youngsters who couldn't understand why I was unable
to play as they did. They began calling me "cross–eyed,"
"four-eyed," and "sissy" because I couldn't compete in
sports. Slowly I retreated into a private little world. A
serious inferiority complex developed, retarding my
growth in many respects for years thereafter.

All through my childhood my parents sought diligently
to find some means of improving my eyes. They took me
to a number of ophthalmologists. When I was sixteen a
doctor recommended surgery for cosmetic purposes only.
It would not improve the eyesight, but would straighten
the crossed eye. The effect of the surgery was only temporary; the left eye soon returned to its abnormal position.

I attended elementary school at St. Anselm's Roman
Catholic Church. Rejected on the playground, embarrassed in the classroom, I sought pleasant refuge in the
church. I loved to sit in the church in the quiet daytime
hours, engrossing its beauty. I absorbed the silent sun's
rays trickling through the sapphire glass windows. I sat in
the empty pews amid the majesty of that lovely building
with its beautiful tapestries and murals and sculpture. The
atmosphere was rich with the varied fragrances of flowers,
incense, and beeswax candles. Especially exhilarating was
the experience of gazing into the sanctuary to meditate and
reflect upon the Eucharist, to gaze at the tabernacle and
feel the presence of our eucharistic Lord. I particularly
enjoyed Sunday mornings, hearing the choir sing all the
beautiful classical chants of the Latin liturgy. And I was
thrilled also to watch the priest stand before the altar
celebrating the drama of our faith in the liturgy of the
mass. As I sat there watching the priest carry out the mass
in sacred sign and symbol, I knew in the very depths of my
heart that's what I wanted to do and that's what I wanted
to be. I believed too it would be the closest in this life I
could possibly be to God, being a priest and consecrating
the elements and bringing forth the Eucharist on the altar.

I would go home from church and try to imitate exactly what the priest did. I made a little altar and spent hours hovering about it. Aunt Mary, a sweet saint who loved God very much, delighted in helping me and encouraging me to become a priest. I knew she loved me dearly, so I approached her about making me a set of liturgical vestments. She agreed. I still recall the anticipation. Just as other children would await a Christmas gift, I waited impatiently for the day Aunt Mary would have my vestments finished. One day she brought a neatly wrapped package. I was so happy. I put on the vestments she made and spent hours with my statues and candles. Whenever they were available, I picked flowers to enhance the beauty of my altar.

When relatives would visit and offer to buy me something, I'd use the money at the ten-cent store or a religious supplies store, always seeking another statue or some other article appropriate for my altar. Every year in school I worked hard to sell the most Christmas seals, for I knew the prize would be some religious gift or statue—another addition to the little altar.

A jack-in-the-box received as a Christmas gift was not really precious until I tore out the clown and covered the box with gold paper and lined the inside. It made a little tabernacle on which I could push a button and the door would fly open. I kept all the "consecrated elements" for communion in that tabernacle. Still—it was too small. So I asked Uncle Julie to make me a tabernacle just like the one they used at church. I gave him the specifications and he obliged. It was much better and bigger than the re-modeled jack-in-the-box.

I have always wanted to be a priest. I believe I was called to proclaim the gospel from the time I was a wink in my father's eye . . . my heavenly Father's eye also. When I was delivered from my mother's womb I think rather than crying I must have said something like *"Dominus vobiscum."* Although my parents were not very religious, they certainly wanted the best for me and for my brother Richard, who was six years older. They arranged for us to go to parochial school. They made certain we attended church services as required by the laws of the Roman Catholic Church. I suppose when they noticed my first inclination toward the priesthood they smiled upon it as child's play. It seems that in the Roman Catholic Church every grade school pupil usually gives some kind of indication that he wants to be a priest or a nun. But my inclinations ran deeper and stronger than most other children. What my parents regarded as child's play was more serious than they realized. They even enjoyed watching me play priest. Going along with the performance, they would sit at my request to witness my celebrating the mass. They would receive the communion (candy wafers or puffed rice) which I offered them. But my parents never spoke a word to encourage me toward the priesthood.

One of my thrilling experiences as a youngster of seven was preparing to receive my own first communion. At that time it was customary for communicants to wear white suits or dresses. I was so excited to be going to the department store to buy my Holy Communion suit. I was so proud. All our relatives came over to visit as I went to church to receive Christ in the Eucharist for the first time. Everyone agreed that I looked like a little angel. I would go to sleep at night with the continuing excitement of knowing that this was merely a foretaste of bigger and more wonderful things to come. This was not simply child's play; I was serious.

After repeated occasions of being humiliated on the playground, I decided it would be much more enjoyable talking to Sister Mary Ellen, who was supervising the school playground. I was fascinated by her dress and the long rosary beads. She was so wonderful; I could ask her questions about God and her answers just thrilled me. It seemed that God had made men, He had made women, and He had made nuns. Nuns were different. Sister Mary Ellen in particular was unlike anyone I knew, a special creation of God.

"What is God like?"

"What do you do when you go back to the big convent?"

"Is it exciting being a nun?"

She was so gentle and considerate to a curious little boy who was suffering complete frustration at normal child's play. Sister Mary Ellen knew everything.

Then one day my mother told us that our cousin Marie Elizabeth was going to be a nun. My very own cousin—a nun! This would be something wonderful to tell Sister Mary Ellen! It even provided me with a brief personal popularity among the other children as I shared this exciting bit of news with them. *My own cousin* is going into the convent! I looked forward to the visiting days at the Divine Providence Mother House in Allison Park.

I tried to get just as close to Marie Elizabeth—now called by her chosen religious name, Sister Maxine—as I did Sister Mary Ellen. Sister Maxine's all-white postulant's dress was the most beautiful I had ever seen. She surely resembled what an angel must look like. Sister and I would walk through the gardens and grottoes together. She would point out the various shrines and statues, telling about each one in detail. For a floundering youngster troubled by his feelings of worthlessness, Sister and I shared one marvelous identity: she would be the first and only nun in the family and I would be the first and only priest in the family! We knew of no one in earlier generations who had chosen these vocations. She would represent my mother's side of the family and I would represent my father's side. We were pioneers, the spiritual giants of the family. Several times a year it was my great joy to visit Sister Maxine, for she was not allowed to come home.

"Is this St. Joseph?" I would ask as we strolled through the gardens.

"Yes."

"Oh, there's the Blessed Mother!"

Sister always had a little gift wrapped for me—a "holy card," rosary beads, or a medal. She instinctively knew exactly what I wanted. The Mother House had a gift shop, and at each visit I would search for just the proper item to improve my lovely altar at home.

We visited our relatives quite often. Jesus said, "Where two or three meet in my name, I shall be there with them." In our large family it seemed that whenever two or three met, the deck of cards would be there with them. All my adult relatives enjoyed playing cards, and they always played for small stakes, such as penny-ante poker. Even so, the winning poker pot seemed like an enormous amount of money to me. This spawned a brilliant idea in my mind. My church still wasn't complete. I got a cigar box, covered it with paper, and cut a slot in the top. Labeling it my church's "poor box," I would sidle up to the aunt or uncle who had just pulled his winnings from the center of the table. With a triumphant laugh, the winner would gladly divide the winnings with the poor.

"Father Mike, here's a little contribution for your church," they said.

At my first opportunity the altar would display another attractive little statue.

One Christmas I received a kit of plaster of Paris molds. The molds were of Indians, soldiers, cowboys, and the like. They were nice, but the kit became much more mean-ingful after I received additional molds of Jesus, St. Joseph, the Blessed Mother, and an angel. I had a booming statue factory, making figurines for sale and for gifts as well as for my own use. I was such a child evangelist that I even recruited some of my Jewish playmates to help paint the statues: "Now these statues are all Jewish people." They were eager to help.

One day my parents took me to a funeral service. As always, I observed carefully everything the priest did. A few days later my father was sleeping on the couch in the family room where I had my altar. My mother walked in to find the lights out, my candles lighted at each end of the couch, a "pall" lying over my father's sleeping body, and his eager eight-year-old son solemnly sprinkling "holy water" over him. The water in his face startled my dad, and he awoke to discover a rosary in his hands. For a split second he wondered, *am I* . . . *?* Quickly he realized that he hadn't yet reached the heavenly gates. Fortunately he found that he hadn't yet reached the heavenly gates. Subsequent family reunions were nearly broken up with laughter as my parents recounted Michael's "funeral service." But little Mike just stood there, piously wondering what was so funny about a "holy" matter.

Next to playing priest, I enjoyed playing school. When I was in the second grade I received a great big blackboard for Christmas. It was so much like the one we had in school. I would stand at the blackboard drawing triangles to represent the Trinity as they taught us in school. I drew crosses and chalices and other signs and symbols we had learned. All I ever wanted to teach my imaginary students was religion. I wasn't interested in learning the multiplication table and other less exciting subjects. One morning I awoke to find the blackboard covered by a large piece of butcher paper. The paper was filled with the entire multiplication table, carefully listed with a black crayon in my father's handwriting. At the bottom he had written a note: "Michael, when you have learned the multiplication table you may play with your blackboard." I could hardly learn it fast enough!

Several years later it was time for Confirmation. We had now moved out to the suburbs of Pittsburgh into a new and better home. But in moving to a new locality we lost some things that were very important to me. Because there was no nearby parochial school, I had to enter public school. I missed the nuns flowing about the classrooms. The atmosphere and decorations of the parochial school were absent in the seemingly bare public school. I longed for the warmth and the comfort and the security of my former school.

Nor could I go to the church any time I wished. It was

two miles away, so I attended only when the other family members did, on Sunday morning. And the suburban church hadn't the same architectural majesty and beauty. It just wasn't as good. It didn't seem as religious. It didn't give the same sense of the presence of God. How I missed *my* church!

Out in the suburbs it was necessary for the priest to hold catechism in scattered homes. Our home was rather large and the priest chose it for the place to hold catechism classes in our community—a new and unexpected thrill! With our sizable basement available, I made it into a veritable church-school. I lined up the chairs, fixed desks, displayed flags, statues, and altars. Even better, after the other students went home, my mother would invite Father Gillian upstairs for refreshments. A priest in our living-room! I listened carefully to every word he spoke about God and I watched and dreamed of the day I too would be a priest.

Thus Confirmation at age twelve became another step closer in my preparation for the priesthood. Confirmation was even more meaningful to me than the other sacraments since the bishop himself was to conduct the service. I was so impressed with his clothing and his regalia. In this sacrament the bishop would lay his hands upon me and impart the sevenfold gifts of the Spirit enumerated in Isaiah 11:2: wisdom, understanding, counsel, fortitude, knowledge, piety, and the fear of the Lord.

I really expected something powerful to occur when the bishop placed his hands upon me. Relatives and friends were in the church to see me walk up to be confirmed. One of my favorite relatives, Uncle John, proudly sponsored me. I returned to my seat happy that I had been confirmed but a little disappointed that I didn't feel anything happen.

2

Preparation and Setbacks

By the time I reached high school I was admitting to myself that I just wasn't a student. Although I still wanted to be a priest, I realized uneasily that the priesthood would require at least eight years of study beyond high school. I had a most difficult time with languages, and Latin was the language of the Church. Our high school Latin teacher had the reputation of being most difficult, so I avoided the course altogether—in spite of the fact that I wanted to be a priest.

A painful adjustment began. As I appraised my life realistically—a poor student, especially poor in languages and afflicted with extremely poor eyesight—I started looking for some other alternative. Others were good at football or good at studies—perhaps I could get a job.

A new shopping center opened near our community. I got a job in an ice cream store that specialized in tall, thin ice cream cones. But the harder I tried to make a tall, thin ice cream cone, the more they came out short and fat. And the young customers inevitably felt cheated. The other boys who worked there were bigger, stronger, more mature —and rougher—than I was. I just felt so weak and frail. So the job lasted less than one month.

I looked around some more. Our family bought all our men's clothing from Allen Lebovitz's men's store. I liked Mr. Lebovitz and I liked his store. I suppose that next to liking the priesthood I liked clothes best. I asked Mr. Lebovitz for a part-time job and he accepted me. Immediately my self-esteem rose; men's clothing was a lot better than ice cream.

Every dollar I earned went into buying more clothes for myself. I was the best-dressed student in the high school. Of all the senior class awards, I was named the best-dressed student of the year—anything to draw attention away from my eyes! I had such a desire for stylish clothing that all the money I earned still couldn't buy enough clothes to satisfy me. I even took money from the cash register to purchase more, and when that seemed too risky, I just settled for selecting what I wanted and walked out of the store with it.

I graduated from high school at nineteen, a year behind my age-group, with a bare minimum of college preparatory courses. My parents wanted me to follow in the footsteps of my older brother who had already completed college. He was everything I wasn't: popular, handsome, athletic. I wore very thick horn-rimmed glasses which tended to disguise the crossed effect. Without the glasses my eyes had a hollow appearance and were very much crossed; therefore I never took off the glasses in public.

But what could I do for a living? I was too frail to do physical work and too weak a student to go much further in school and my eyesight was too poor to depend upon it. I did enjoy my part-time job selling men's clothing and I was actually quite good at it. Perhaps I could remain in some form of retailing. But my parents continued to urge college upon me.

A new junior college, Robert Morris, had just been founded in Pittsburgh. They needed students and I needed a college that would accept me. We welcomed each other. They took a personal interest in each student; I was a worthwhile individual there. Perhaps a business course, looking ahead to a future in retailing, would be what I should take. The school insisted upon their students dressing in a businesslike manner and that was the best thing I could do. None of the irritating nicknames followed from public school; nobody picked on me because I couldn't defend myself. The "Father Mike" label my relatives had given me as a child was seldom heard any more. I began to feel almost like a junior executive, going downtown each day in my stylish clothes, carrying an important-looking attache case. None of the professors could compare me with my older brother. And by the wonderful grace of God I began to enjoy school for the first time in my life.

I absorbed the warm acceptance among the faculty and administration. Further, I enjoyed all the subjects and gradually became a confident student. I was well-liked among both faculty and students. I became advertising manager of the college paper, then general manager, and eventually editor! I joined a fraternity because my grades were so good and later became eligible to join an honorary fraternity because I had made the dean's list. I sang in the glee club and became treasurer of the student council. Everyday I was able to attend mass at St. Peter's downtown. By taking summer classes I completed a three-year program in two years and graduated with honors. Life was becoming much more satisfying. An opportunity to work in public relations and advertising was offered immediately upon graduation.

My parents were perhaps more excited about my future than I was. While they were away on vacation I attended a layman's retreat at St. Vincent's College in thanksgiving to God for my successful completion of junior college. I was also asking God for help in my future business career. It was the first retreat I had ever made. During the retreat God spoke to me in my spirit. I could feel a gentle nudging: the priesthood. I spoke to Him too: "Lord, it has always been academics that have blocked my becoming a priest. Now that you have shown me that I can do well in college, I'm willing to give the priesthood a try." For I knew that no matter how successful I was in business, I wouldn't be happy unless I gave my first love an opportunity to come to fruition. I made the decision then and there.

I returned home from the retreat excited. When my parents' vacation was ended I gushed, "Oh, I have such wonderful news for you!"

They of course assumed it was the confirmation of my new job: the salary would be high and the opportunities excellent.

I told them my good news and their faces dropped. They were shocked and disappointed. For one thing, they felt I would be biting off more than I could chew, venturing into those difficult studies just after having completed my business degree. My dad was a welder, working very hard for a living, and from his practical viewpoint he was surely wondering about the loss of his investment in my business education. Although my parents weren't pleased about it, they gave me their blessing. They always wanted for their two sons whatever would make us happy.

I have been asked about my feelings concerning the priesthood, celibacy, and various personal disciplines and sacrifices. Actually, there never was a feeling of sacrifice for me. I always knew that priests and nuns were set apart by God as very special persons. I was *privileged* to announce that I was going to be a priest! I have simply been in love with my heavenly Father for as long as I can remember. It is difficult for me to understand why *everyone* doesn't love Him. Celibacy is no sacrifice to one who feels what I have always felt. I know I could marry and be happy, but marriage would have a distinct effect upon this feeling of being set apart and very special. As I ponder the lives of some of the early Christians—St. Paul, St. Cyprian, St. Origen—they seem to have felt the same way about their vocations. It was a wonderful blessing just to be called to be a priest.

The decision to enter the priesthood was more easily made than accomplished. There were three major stumbling blocks. First, the Church wanted candidates for the priesthood to be in as nearly perfect health as possible. My eyes of course would present a difficulty in passing the medical requirement. Second, I had no Latin; many seminary textbooks were in Latin. Third, an undergraduate degree in philosophy was required before the Roman Catholic Church would enroll a candidate in theology. Very few of my business courses would be acceptable to the seminary, which meant taking quite a lot of undergraduate prerequisite courses in philosophy and classics before enrolling in a seminary.

But I felt the call of God upon my life so strongly that I was certain He wished me to be a priest. I knew that, like St. Paul, "God, who had specially chosen me . . . and called me through His grace," would open all the doors. Immediately I enrolled in Duquesne University to study Latin, philosophy, and an undergraduate course in theology. I also began making application to various dioceses and seminaries.

Duquesne University started out to be exciting too. I had learned to love studying although the Latin was difficult and I just barely passed the course. I could continue to attend mass every day, now right on campus. I was rubbing elbows with priests and sisters and Catholic students. The old nickname, "Father Mike," began to reappear when uncles and aunts gathered. The social and religious life of the University was pleasant indeed, but the Latin weighed heavily upon me. Memorizing vocabulary, conjugating verbs, and declining nouns were drudgery. My Latin vocabulary cards became a familiar sight. Standing at the bus stop, I would be riffling through the vocabulary cards, trying to memorize the Latin words in spite of an apparent mental block. The cards would be seen beside my plate at mealtime, in the bathroom—whenever I might seize a minute to study. Friends and relatives looked askance at me when I would pick up the words to study them momentarily during the few seconds between hands of a card game.

Meanwhile, the negative replies began coming from diocesan offices and from the seminaries. Some felt it was my eyes; others noted my Latin deficiency; still others thought my high school grades demonstrated an inability to handle seminary, and just because I had good grades in business school didn't necessarily mean that I could comprehend philosophy and other related courses. In addition to my lack of academic college courses there arose an unexpected problem: I was twenty-two years old and candidates for the priesthood are expected to be in seminary at that age. I hadn't even finished my first year of Latin yet. They called mine a "belated vocation."

Each negative reply provided the occasion for another traumatic scar upon a life which had already known so much rejection and disappointment. The applications were all so complicated. Each one required copies of my baptismal and confirmation certificates, my parents' marriage certificate, a medical report from our family doctor, and letters of recommendation from our pastor and other appropriate persons. After each denial from a seminary I had to accumulate the same forms to include with the application to the next seminary on my list. It was so embarrassing and humiliating to have to return time after time to the particular individuals, asking for an identical letter or document. The seminaries all had the policy of never returning the application.

Then the ever present question, "Why do you want to be a priest?" To this day I have not discovered the correct answer—if there is a correct answer. With each application I gave a different reply to that question, hoping to stumble upon the magic words. I thought to myself, "What I wrote before didn't work, so this time I'll try something new." I used every approach imaginable. I tried sounding pious—then I got psychological—then humanitarian. One time I really thought I had found the correct handle.

"Since I have specialized in business school in public relations and advertising, I want to be a public relations man for Christ," I wrote. That didn't work either.

I labored long over every application—examining, rewriting, and polishing. Being so certain that God wanted me to be a priest, I would only apply to one seminary at a time. Surely this is the one! After several weeks the tension would build within me. My parents began to share my pain and anxiety. I tried to get to the mailbox first in order to read the letter privately when it arrived. I could always tell from the first few words that a rejection was coming. The letters were always so gracious and kind. The typical response is indelibly impressed upon my mind:

Dear Michael,

We are aware of your desire and eagerness to be a priest, and we appreciate your efforts to be of service to our diocese. But we deeply regret however, that after reviewing your academic record, we believe it is not the will of God that you study for the priesthood at this time. Perhaps in the years to come God will make it possible for you to pursue the vocation of your choice.

If we can be of any service or assistance to you, kindly inform us. Please be assured of our prayers.

Sincerely yours in Christ,
Director of Vocations

I suppose there is no diplomatic way to break someone's heart. No matter how delicately they tried to say it, each time the pain was so great I could hardly bear it. This repeated cycle of application and rejection went on for more than two years!

One particular application I decided would be the final attempt. I refused to apply again. *God has got to produce this time!* I thought. But it too brought a negative reply. I locked myself in my room. I was so depressed that I was considering suicide. Only my fear of eternal damnation prevented it. Even then, the utter rejection and its accompanying pain seemed almost as bad as everlasting punishment.

After a few hours my parents knocked on the door. I wouldn't answer. A couple of hours later they knocked again, then tried the door to find it locked. I didn't want to talk to anyone! I heard their concerned voices outside the room, but I kept my face buried in a bed full of tears. They realized that I must have received another letter of rejection.

They said, "Michael, we love you. We'll love you whether you're a priest or not!"

Finally I assured them I was alive by blurting out, "Go away!"

After some time they asked one of my favorite neighbors, Clara, to try to reason with me. Clara was quite persuasive, but I resisted with another pitiful "Go away!"

I spent about twenty-four hours in my room, going to the bathroom only on the several occasions when I heard my parents go across the street to see the neighbors. At last I pulled myself together and came out to try to resume normal life. And once again I applied to still another seminary.

3

Dream Becomes Reality

For some time I had been attempting to demonstrate my willingness to do whatever was necessary to become a priest. In order to win the favor of the Church I had accepted a teaching position in a parochial elementary school. As I taught fourth, fifth, and sixth grades, I seemed able to relive my own grade school years vicariously. Many of the things I missed as a youngster I tried to impart to my students. We had a happy classroom. Together we enjoyed decorating the room as beautifully and attractively as we could.

And of course there was the ever-enjoyable religious life —mass every morning. I loved the pastor dearly; he was a good man. My favorite course, as always, was religion. I taught the children all about the sacramental life of the Church. Since I had enjoyed playing priest so much, I assumed that these youngsters would too. So we built a little altar in the classroom. A Mary altar, with devotions to Mary, is a common parochial school custom. But earlier in the year we built a larger, eucharistic altar which I used to teach the children all about the mass as we built it. As a religious class project we reenacted the entire mass. A number of the boys wanted to play priest, so their mothers made vestments for them as Aunt Mary had made them for me so many years before. We had all the things which a priest would have on the altar and I taught the children the mass in Latin. As they learned to pronounce the Latin, I was learning it better too. After working all year on this project, our fourth-grade class presented it for the entire school. We presented not only the mass, but the benediction as well. In the benediction the Eucharist would be put in a monstrance and the priest would bless the people with the consecrated elements. It included various songs and prayers and then the final benediction with the Eucharist. The school principal allowed us to enact this for the parents. The youngsters were thrilled with the opportunity. Every member of the class had a part in it and they were quite conscientious in fulfilling their roles. I was very proud of them, and of course I was reliving some of my childhood as well as learning more about the finer points of the mass myself.

Thus I assumed I would be accepted in seminary after this. I had done a good job. But the rejections continued. So I returned to teaching, this time in high school.

Ironically, I was accepted to teach at St. Anselm's, the same school in which I had failed the first grade. This was a good school academically and the position paid more. I taught religion along with the other courses. Again I taught the students all about the sacramental life and teachings of the Church and the commandments of God. I was learning more and more about the religious life through closer fellowship with the priests and nuns of the parish. The prescribed classroom discipline was difficult for me to maintain. I tried to enjoy my students and have them enjoy me. I was a successful teacher, but still I failed in many ways to come to terms with myself and my identity. But then, teaching was merely temporary—not a career, a means to an end only.

Just a few weeks after I had emphatically declared that I would never apply to another seminary, I was reading in a magazine: *"It's Never Too Late To Become A Priest!"* It was an advertisement by a seminary for belated vocations. By now I was twenty-four years old.

"Maybe that's the one for me." And it was! To my amazement and joy, they accepted me!

Holy Apostles Seminary was located in Cromwell, Connecticut. I left home for the first time in my life. Mom and Dad and my very thrilled godparents drove me to Connecticut. My parents hated leaving me there, assuming I wouldn't like it. They were sure I'd be home on the next train. But my godparents were confident that I would persevere. "After all, Michael is *our* godson!" they said.

As Mom and Dad anticipated, the excitement began to disappear as soon as they drove off. Pittsburgh was so far away and I could not go home until Christmas. Could I stay away from those I loved that long? I went to my room. It was so small, so bare, so depressing. No drapes, no carpet —just a bare mattress and a bare dresser. I sat down and cried. Growing up hurts sometimes.

Yet I *was* happy. My seminary career had finally begun! The older students made all of us new students feel welcome and I went to work. I was very conscientious, very scrupulous, very zealous. I tried to do everything exactly the way the professors would tell me to do it. You might say that I was a model seminarian. Many classes were quite enjoyable—humanities, the arts—all except Latin! Ten hours of Latin class time each week and I hated every minute of it. The priest who taught it was a good and likable man, but that didn't make me enjoy it one bit. I dreamed on long walks through the countryside of how wonderful it would be when these years were finished and I would be ordained a priest.

At the close of two years at Holy Apostles I was prepared

to go on to what is called "major seminary" to complete philosophy courses and to study theology. In the Roman Catholic Church a candidate for the priesthood must be sponsored by a bishop before he can be enrolled in a major seminary. I applied to various dioceses and was accepted by the bishop of the Diocese of Steubenville, Ohio. I was so grateful to the bishop for his warm acceptance of me, and I enrolled in St. John Vianney Seminary of Bloomingdale, Ohio. Now it was just a matter of a few more years!

My seminaries had names with which I could easily identify. The first holy apostles were men who had secular vocations but were called out by Jesus. In my own case there was the degree in business and the fact that I had entered seminary later than most of those who aspire to the priesthood. Long after I had given up on the priesthood the Lord called me back to my original plan. St. John Vianney also was a man with whom I could identify. He was a young man of the eighteenth century—a youth who was determined at all costs to fulfill the vocation of priest. He had a difficult time with languages and was an especially poor Latin student. But he struggled to the completion of his studies. St. John later became an outstanding confessor—a man who had a very special compassion and love for lost, troubled, burdened, or sin-sick souls. Multitudes of people flocked to him for confession and counsel. With his help many were able to find the peace of God through the sacrament of Confession. St. John Vianney was an inspiring example to a young man who suffered from the same language difficulties, but who was determined to find his vocation in the priesthood. How many times during my language struggles I would think about him and plunge back to my studies with a fierce determination!

One Christmas I was invited to participate in the midnight liturgy at St. Mary's Church, where I had taught elementary school six years before. This was to be my first church function as an ordained cleric in a church near home. I dressed in my black cassock, with black socks and black shoes, put on my black topcoat and black biretta, even adding the black gloves. Before we left the house for St. Mary's, my parents stopped to look at me. They smiled, and I smiled. Tears welled up in my mother's eyes. We drove to the church, where I stood for a period in the lobby, greeting uncles, aunts, and cousins who had forsaken their home parishes this night to see Michael participate in the mass. A number of my former pupils—now high school students—flocked around me to offer their wisecracking congratulations. Hugged, kissed, and cried over, I was *"our* Michael!"

The Christmas liturgy was beautiful. In this special situation I was permitted to wear the vestments of a subdeacon. What a thrill to be part of such a glorious celebration with all its awesome pageantry! There I was, functioning at the altar with the pastor and assistant pastor— my own personal heroes—in a church packed with relatives and friends, many of whom had come just to see me participate.

Proudest of all were Aunt Barb and Uncle Bob. Perhaps most dedicated of all my relatives, I feel they would have been outstanding as a nun and a priest had they not chosen holy matrimony. Throughout my seminary years Aunt Barb and Uncle Bob visited me, wrote often, and prayed daily for my progress. Aunt Barb baked cookies and mended my cassocks with a dedicated diligence. She wanted me to look perfect!

After we went home I spent the remainder of the night lying awake in bed, aglow with a continuing excitement. In the morning the same thrill carried over into my home parish as I also assisted in the Christmas mass at St. Regis Church.

During the summers of seminary years I worked as a camp counselor in a Jesuit boys' camp in Lenox, Massachusetts. I always remained as close as I could to the priest and the chapel at camp. To be selected to work with Jesuits was a religious status symbol. I would discuss with the priest almost endlessly the spiritual life and the deeper aspects of theology.

Once the youngsters even mocked me in a skit by ringing a little bell and announcing to everybody, "Chapel tours! Chapel tours! Chapel tours!" Everybody howled with laughter. I was furious! I knew the other counselors had inspired that mockery, and I resented it. I felt like a martyr for the faith.

That was absolutely sacrilegious! They are undermining all the values I'm trying to impart to these boys! I thought. I couldn't even laugh at myself.

I could not learn enough about God. I know now that I was born with an immense hunger for Him. My spiritual appetite has been almost insatiable. From the age of five I could sense the personal presence of God. I loved Jesus. In fact, I cannot recall a time as a boy when I did not know the joy of salvation. To this day I still want to devour the Scriptures, to devour the instructions of competent Christian teachers. I love to study about God. Spiritual matters may be boring to some, but to me as a child and even to me today, they are a continuing series of exciting discoveries. Only a brief period of agnosticism toward the end of my seminary days has ever interrupted my love for God and all the things of God.

I completed my studies in philosophy at St. John Vianney and then began theology. I thought, *Now in theology I'm going to learn more and more about God and get closer and closer to Him.*

Theological studies were concentrated in liturgy, dogma, doctrine, moral theology, homiletics, Scripture, and canon law. At the end of the first year I received my tonsure. In past centuries the candidate would be completely shaved on the back of the head to show his being set apart for the priesthood. Today the bishop merely clips a bit of hair symbolically and ordains the candidate a cleric. So the day after I received my tonsure I was ordained to minor orders. The first two minor orders of the church are porter and lector. A porter can open the doors of the church and has custody of the keys and the property. A lector teaches and reads the Scripture during the liturgy.

But theology didn't cause me to know God better. It didn't draw me closer to Him. In fact, a gap appeared and that gap began to widen. The study of theology can have this effect, particularly upon one who is expecting such study to bring him closer to God. By the time I had completed two years of theology, God was less real to me than when I had begun. I found myself going into chapel for prayer, for morning laudes, and for vespers and compline, and being unmoved, unstirred, untouched by the prayers and the liturgy of the chapel service. I would walk out feeling empty. I was frustrated with my lack of growth. Although I looked all right externally, I knew that I still had the same jealousies, the same hang-ups, the same hatreds, the same resentments, the same bitterness. No matter what kind of religious apparel I would put on and no matter how I would appear to someone else, I knew in my heart what I was, and I was quite dissatisfied with it. It is agonizing to recall those painful feelings. I became more and more disappointed with myself.

As I studied theology I could quote Barth, Tillich, Bultmann, Rahner, Schillebeeckx, and countless other theologians, but that didn't change me or make Jesus Christ any more real in my life.

There is a story told about a number of theologians meeting to discuss Christology—who Jesus is. These theologians were presenting papers and holding discussions among themselves with the expectation of publishing the results of their symposium. Suddenly Jesus Himself appeared among them and asked the same question He asked of the Twelve: "Who do you say that I am?"

A spokesman for the group stood up and said, "You are the eschatological manifestation of the ground of being, the kerygma manifested in the humanizing process."

With a puzzled look Jesus replied, "Who?"

During those years of studying theology, the great difference between what I wanted to be and what I really was became more and more apparent. I would go to confession every week, even several times a week, confessing the same repeated sins and weaknesses. Kneeling to say penance, I would feel tears of frustration streaming down my face. I needed so much for someone to remind me that I had been saved by the grace of God who loved me. I would share my anguish with students and professors in private discussions and counseling sessions. They would try to help, but I seemed unable to communicate my feelings to them. I was becoming more divided, wanting the priesthood, yet more painfully aware of my sins than ever before. Seminary by now was simply boring. The same routine—day after day, week after week, month after month! It was all so mechanical, conforming to rules and regulations. I couldn't seem to articulate my concern about my own unrighteousness, and so most of the struggle remained bottled up within me. Finally I staggered to a terrible conclusion.

It may be a difficult decision to make when one enters the priesthood. The decision to leave is a thousand times more difficult. During my years of study I saw many young men come to seminary hoping they had a vocation to the priesthood, but after spending a year or two found out they didn't. Never in my wildest imaginations did I dream that one day I might join their ranks. The very thought of it frightened me and I found myself tossing and turning at night. Should I stay or should I leave? I just knew I couldn't go on being the hypocrite that I was. I couldn't go on when I was entertaining all these doubts about whether God existed or whether Christ was actually the Son of God. My head was so full of confusion, theology, and philosophy. I just couldn't put it all together. And then one day I read these words on a bumper sticker: "If God seems absent from your life, guess who moved!"

God may have been there all right, but I found myself turning away from Him more and more. I no longer desired to pray. I began to turn in my thoughts to the world and the things of the world and the ways of the world. Why did I forsake a successful business career just to come to seminary? I could be out making a lot of money and driving a big car and doing a lot of other exciting things. I made a mistake. I was taking pills at night to put me to sleep and taking pills in the daytime to keep me awake. I just couldn't go on this way! What had happened to me?

Finally, in December 1969, with less than two years of seminary and a year of internship before ordination to the priesthood, I came to a painful decision. I announced to my spiritual director, to the Seminary Rector, and to my fellow students that I was leaving the seminary. Perhaps my superiors should have rejoiced. I had become quite a problem for them. In my frustration I had become bitter and apathetic.

I asked for a year's leave of absence. I wanted the understanding that after I left, if things were to change or if I could come to terms with myself and God, I could return to seminary and continue again after a year out of school. And if there was no change of heart, I would just forget about the priesthood entirely. I thought I would go home for the Christmas holidays and simply announce to my family and friends that I wasn't returning to school. The seminary officials encouraged me to finish the school year. I knew they were looking out for my best interests, so I returned to seminary after Christmas. As soon as I arrived I knew I shouldn't have come. January to May was such a long time—it seemed interminable. Because I would be leaving with two years of theology yet to complete, I did not receive the scheduled ordination to second minor orders in January of that year.

But I was glad to be out. Suddenly I felt free to do what I wished instead of being required to follow the dull routine of seminary life. Yet I was also sad. I had let down so many people who had encouraged me and prayed for me all those years. And I knew I was running from God. I hated to look in the mirror every day and realize that I wasn't the man I thought I was; I had tossed in the towel when things became dull and monotonous.

4

A New Mike

With this attitude of mixed feelings I accepted a position teaching psychology at a small business school in Pittsburgh one week after leaving seminary. Very quickly I began thinking of psychology as if it had all the answers I needed for myself. I wondered, *What makes me tick? Why do I respond in certain ways in certain situations? What causes me to react like that?* I found myself presenting psychology to the students the way a minister would proclaim the Word of God. I was making it my Bible as I began applying it so extensively to my own life. I was using psychology to answer the needs of students and friends who would confide their problems to me.

Although I was teaching as a layman, by the third week some of the students learned I had been preparing for the priesthood. They thought that since I was going to be a priest I would be interested in attending a prayer meeting. At that time a prayer meeting was the last thing I was interested in. I was not only taking a leave of absence from seminary, but also a leave of absence from all religious activity. I felt that the further I got from the Church and its activities, the more objectively I could look at my vocation. But because of my love for my students I agreed to go.

The prayer meeting was held in the nurses' recreation room of Shadyside Hospital. About eighty students from various schools and universities all over Pittsburgh were present. Some of these colleges are well-known for their agnosticism and atheism and yet these students were praising the Lord and giving testimonies to what God was doing in their lives. They were studying the Scriptures together too. I thought, *How odd that undergraduate students would gather this way, since their normal behavior at this time in life is to want to break away from home, church, and the Establishment.* These were most unusual students. Being the skeptic I was at that time, I began to analyze the whole situation. *What is their motivation for being here? Perhaps this is simply a crutch: they are social outcasts or wallflowers. Or perhaps they have nothing else to do and they can't get dates.*

But I made the mistake of looking around. *These kids are handsome and beautiful. And they're here* with *their dates. Well, maybe they're planning on going into the priesthood or the ministry or some form of church work.* Then I discovered that they were majoring in law, medicine, engineering, pharmacy, education, and political science—not one was planning to enter seminary. And I couldn't pray the way they were praying. I could have devised a prayer easily enough, but I couldn't have prayed with the same sincerity, with the same assurance.

When the prayer meeting ended, we all went out to a restaurant for refreshments. Now, I thought, they'll start talking shop—law or medicine or professors or tennis or roommates or dating. But they just continued talking about the Lord. I thought if I heard them say "Praise the Lord!" one more time, I'd choke. They seemed to sense that there was something amiss in my spirit, but out of love and respect they wouldn't embarrass me. No one grabbed me and asked, "Brother, are you saved?" Nor did anyone demand, "Have you been immersed?" or, "Have you been filled with the Holy Ghost?" nor even, "Can I straighten out your theology?" They just loved me. The divine love—*agape*—flowed from them to me. No one can argue with love. I couldn't resist it. I found myself returning to their prayer meetings week after week. And I didn't even want to go. I was being loved back to life!

One July Sunday afternoon I just wished to be alone. I wanted to think and relax, so I went to a movie. I loved the theatre and opera, and I have always received pleasure from the movies. But after this particular show I was left with an empty, lonely feeling. I didn't want to go home yet; the day seemed quite incomplete.

Well, what can I do now? Maybe I could go visit Allen Lebovitz and his family.

I drove all the way to their house, but they weren't home. The empty, lonely feeling increased to irritability: *Why aren't they home? Whom can I visit now? What am I going to do?*

Someone had told me about a Sunday evening prayer meeting in a church near the Lebovitzes. I knew that church well. I used to play around it as a small boy when I visited my Aunt Margaret and Uncle Harry who lived nearby. Because it was Protestant I had never dared enter the church. Now I racked my brain for someone to visit or something else to do. This prayer meeting was the only thing I could think of. I drove around the community for some time, then finally headed for the church. It was called the Pittsburgh Church of the Brethren.

I had a difficult time finding a parking place; there were cars parked everywhere. Dressed in an anonymous sport shirt, I walked in as the service was about to begin. I sat in a folding chair back near the door because I had heard about some strange things that went on in *that church.*

But as the meeting began, I experienced immediately the same enthusiasm, the same love, the same joy, the same testimonies of how Jesus is still alive. This often-repeated statement that Jesus is alive was so new to me. The atmosphere was almost electric, and I sensed again the feelings I had felt at the college prayer meeting.

Pastor Russ Bixler said, "Let's introduce ourselves. How many Presbyterians are here? How many Methodists?" As each denomination stood up, everyone applauded.

"If he mentions Roman Catholics, I thought, I'll be the only one. Maybe I shouldn't stand up." But there were many Catholics. I was so shocked I almost forgot to stand up myself. Suddenly I felt comfortable. I felt at ease although it was obvious that these people had something I didn't have. They had a freedom, a power that was beyond themselves. And I was hungry for it.

As all these Christians lifted their hands in worship, they began to sing, each in a different language. None of the tongues were intelligible to me, yet it was like a symphony orchestra, with all the various instruments playing at the same time. It was as if there were a conductor leading the musicians and all the languages were blending into one beautiful orchestral whole, a lovely symphonic offering of praise. The singing would diminish into a soft hush, then like a billow coming in from the ocean another wave of praise would mount up and swell and spill over into the next crescendo of worship and praise. Even if I didn't understand what was going on, I knew God was there. And I knew that something exciting and real and wonderful was taking place. My memory was nudged with an image of seminary days at Holy Apostles. I couldn't translate the Latin chants as rapidly as we sang them, but I always enjoyed a thrilling experience of worship as we sang the Divine Office. We would practice for weeks each year for the Easter liturgy. Many of the seminarians had well-trained voices; consequently the Easter liturgy was an exquisitely beautiful musical presentation. Yet here in this church I was hearing unrehearsed singing in the Spirit which was just as beautiful and moving as what we had worked so hard to develop in seminary.

At some point during this beautiful worship I cried out, "Lord, restore to me the joy of my salvation! Do for me what I can't do for myself! Bless me as you have blessed these people here!"

When the meeting ended, I stood up and walked out the door. Halfway down the steps I stopped abruptly. I was hungry in my heart. I was attracted by this "something" these people had. They had somehow tapped The Source. I was drawn like a moth to the light. I wanted to open up, to surrender, to receive. As I look back, there was no orderly pattern or logic to my thoughts. Every good thing was simply converging upon me—some thoughts conscious, some surely unconscious. I was not fully aware of what I was doing. I am more of a *feeling* person than a thinking person. At least I had to return to inquire; to that extent I was thinking logically.

I turned quickly and strode deliberately all the way up the aisle to the front of the church. There was only one vacant chair in a long row. I sat on it before I paused to realize what I was doing. The pastor was giving instructions to those who wished to receive the baptism in the Holy Spirit. Because of the great peace that was settling over me, I was hardly listening. He prayed for us all, gave further instructions, and gleefully told us to expect things to be different.

I have often tried to analyze the events of that evening. I have asked myself, "What really happened?" I didn't realize until days later that God had actually baptized me in the Holy Spirit while I was worshiping during the service. I was crying out to the Lord to restore the joy of my salvation. I began to sing with the congregation, to take an active part in that beautiful symphony of praise. With my hands raised in adoration, I too was praising the Lord in a new language—singing in the Spirit with every-

one else—so caught up in the beauty and love and glory
of God that I surrendered to Him without being con-
sciously aware of it. The "tongues" just seemed to be a
normal, unobtrusive part of the whole experience of worship. But only in subsequent weeks did much of that experience take objective shape in my memory.

That night I slept better than any night for a long time.
The hungry, gnawing incomplete feeling was gone. The
day was more than complete. As the days passed, I found
that much of the anxiety, tension, worry about the future,
guilt about the past, depression, fear, loneliness, and
doubts whether God exists or whether He loves me or
whether Christ is the Son of God no longer haunted me.
There was no human being who explained my experience
to me that I might know what was occurring. I merely
lived these experiences. I found a great freedom, a great
joy, a great optimism about life and about the future.
Jesus was so real!

My students began to recognize the change in me. As
part of a psychology project, I had given the students the
opportunity to make a five-minute talk on any subject related to psychology. Many of the students had selected subjects such as ESP, seances, palm reading, yoga, handwriting
analysis, and the like. Whereas I had formerly been keenly
interested in such matters, they now all seemed so shallow
and trite. I could recognize as the students spoke that truth
was being perverted. I could now distinguish these occult
errors from truth. It seemed each day that the Lord was re-
vealing more and more of Himself to me. I was walking
more and more in His light. The Scriptures were taking
on the dimension of good news; it really was good and it
really was news. It wasn't something old, just from 2,000
years ago. It was current enough that I could relate it to
life today. Many Scriptures took on new meaning, and instead of an obligation it was a pleasure to read the Bible.
New light was dawning upon me: this Book is replete with
the supernatural! It's loaded with the direct dealings of

God with man! Now philosophy and psychology were dry and the Scriptures enjoyable—a complete reversal within two brief months!

More and more I was discerning right and wrong as the students continued giving their five-minute talks. I could see so clearly the difference between the light of the gospel and the powers of darkness manifested in seances, horoscopes, fortune-telling, and other occult practices.

I was hearing testimonies at all the meetings I attended of physical healings. One day I was window-shopping downtown during my lunch hour. I stopped before a Christian Science Reading Room display. Healing was mentioned there, so I went inside. The lady told me of their work and suggested that I attend a service. I did. I heard testimonies of alleged healings, each one ending something like this: "I'm very grateful to Christian Science for my healing."

I'd never heard that before. In other meetings it was usually, "I'm very grateful to Jesus for my healing." And the joy was not in evidence in the Christian Science Church. I began to wonder about it.

A few days later I stopped in the Reading Room on my lunch hour again and opened my Bible to read. "If you're going to read here, it must be some of *our* literature," I was emphatically told.

"But I was reading the Bible. Isn't that appropriate here?"

"No. I'm sorry, but the Reading Room is only for Christian Science literature."

That did it. God let me know very quickly whose side they were on. He was teaching me so rapidly!

Another fascinating—even startling—change was taking place within me. With each passing week I felt a stronger urge to go back into the work of the Church on a full-time basis. I didn't want to be involved in psychology; I wanted to be involved in ministry. Although psychology contains truth, it is only a small portion in the light of the full truth of the gospel. Only two months after I had left seminary in darkness and despair, I was eager to preach the good news again. It was as if someone had turned on a high-powered floodlight into the gloom in which I had been walking. I prayed, asking the Lord to get me out of the psychology class and into a ministry for the Lord.

I was told that St. Perpetua's Church had just built a new educational center and they needed someone to be its administrator and CCD (Confraternity of Christian Doctrine) director. So I went to the church and spoke to the pastor and presented my credentials. He was impressed by my experience and education, so he offered me a part-time position.

There is an old Portuguese saying: "God writes straight with crooked lines." Many of the things I had done in my life appeared so unrelated to each other. Some experiences seemed so useless. Yet when I began this job, I discovered that all my varied qualifications were needed. The job required administrative abilities; I had received that training in my business education. Many in the congregation had to be sold on the possibilities the new educational center could hold for the parish; I had sales experience and had done rather well in it. The job needed teaching experience; I had done that also. The job required a director who was trained in Vatican II theology (that is, since Pope John XXIII); all my seminary training had taken place since then, so it had included Vatican II theology. But most of all, I had received the baptism in the Holy Spirit and the Spirit was empowering everything I did in Jesus' name.

I soon found myself talking to the young people about the love of Jesus Christ and presenting the gospel with a newfound effectiveness. I was teaching youngsters spontaneous prayer and they were enjoying it. I began to teach things I was learning in some Bible study classes that I had been attending. The young people started worshiping spontaneously in the CCD assemblies. They would go home and tell their parents how much they enjoyed their experiences at the religious education center. Repeatedly parents would mention with genuine excitement how different their children were. "And they are singing about God all the time they're working at their chores!"

I was attending prayer meetings all over the Pittsburgh area. It mattered little whether they were Catholic or Protestant; I was hungry for all of God I could get!

Some folks are "day people." They awake early and are most productive in the daytime. Others are "night people," staying up late and dragging themselves through the morning hours. I have always been a "day" person, retiring around ten or eleven P.M. The Catholic Church has always pleased me in this respect because I enjoy early morning worship. After the baptism in the Holy Spirit I began coming home at one or one-thirty A.M. Most prayer meetings I attended were in the evening, and with the anointing of the Spirit everyone would seem to lose track of time. The meetings just went on and on and nobody seemed to care. This little ditty rings with truth:

> Mary had a little lamb which never grew to be a sheep;
> It became a Pentecostal and died from lack of sleep.

Formerly these late hours would have left me exhausted, but I continued to bubble and exude energy and interest in all activities. My parents were becoming concerned. "Where have you been?"

"Oh, at a prayer meeting" (or, "a Bible study").

They didn't say much more, but they were wondering. After all, nobody prays that late. "Does Michael have a girl friend?"

Before the baptism in the Holy Spirit I just couldn't bear Oral Roberts, Kathryn Kuhlman, or Rex Humbard. They were so foolish, so—Protestant! Now I was listening to their programs while I was getting dressed to go to mass. "Is Michael becoming a Protestant?" my family wondered.

Because the nuns were beginning to wear modified

dresses, even street clothes, I wondered why priests and seminarians couldn't switch from their black clothing too. So I bought a gray suit. Each time I dressed in the gray suit, my parents would laugh: "Oh, Michael's going to a Protestant church again!"

I have always loved my parents deeply. They have been good to me. Yet I see imperfections in them. The imperfections, however, don't make me love my parents any less. This is analogous to my love for Holy Mother Church, the Roman Catholic Church. I have always loved the Church and submitted to her authority, but I still see her imperfections and her weaknesses. The baptism in the Holy Spirit has deepened my love and concern for the Church, and it has added new depth to the word "catholic," which means "universal."

The Holy Spirit has so broadened my understanding of this universality of the Church that I can now appreciate and receive blessing from a Protestant church service. He is creating supernaturally what we humans have only considered nostalgically—a genuine ecumenical movement in the churches. The whole picture reminds me of a tossed salad: lettuce, radishes, tomatoes, endive, cucumbers—Catholics, Methodists, Baptists, Episcopalians. But the salad does not blend together until "the dressing" —the Holy Spirit—is added to make it a tasty union of distinctive flavors.

Although I had known the Lord personally since early childhood, the baptism in the Holy Spirit sharpened my awareness of that wonder of wonders: personal salvation by the grace of God in Jesus Christ. I was now realizing in a much more objective way all that had happened to me years before. Every good thing—walking by faith in Jesus, being justified by His blood, experiencing the love of God daily—was deepening in my conscious mind. I felt saturated with His love. And now I was able to see more clearly what had actually occurred when I believed in Jesus as a youngster.

I also learned at this time that the word Pentecost ends with "cost." There *is* a price to pay for being baptized in the Holy Spirit. Discipleship has been defined as "an invitation to die." As my psychology students continued their five-minute talks on the occult, I began referring more and more to what I was experiencing—the power of God to heal a person's emotional problems and warning of the terrible dangers of the occult world. I told the students how my long hours with the psychologist at Duquesne University and extensive counseling in seminary had made me quite aware of my emotional problems, yet left me still powerless to overcome those problems. I pointed out that Jesus was a Healer, and the students loved these discussions. But some of the administration overheard snatches of my classes and they called me in, explaining that they didn't want to lose their reputation as a good business school. I was promptly dismissed, not even being allowed to return to the classroom, but quickly ushered out the front door. Several students standing near the door tried to ask me what was going on, but I was sternly ordered not to speak to them. And the door slammed shut.

In my earlier years such an experience would have been a trauma; I would have been crushed. I went to the parking lot and got in my car. "Lord! You honored my prayer to get me out of the psychology class, but did You have to do it so violently?!"

Rather than feeling sorry for myself I began quietly praying in tongues. As I thus prayed in the Spirit, a tremendous sense of confidence and joy swept over me. I knew suddenly that God was somehow involved in my dismissal and that it would become a dismissal into better things. I just knew that all things do indeed work together for good for those who love God.

I was concerned however about my parents' reaction. My mother is like a detective: she knows instinctively when something is wrong. While I was still pondering how to break the news to them, Mom looked right at me and unloaded. "You've been fired, haven't you? That wouldn't have happened if you had kept your mouth shut!"

She was right. I had enjoyed the job; the salary was the best I had ever known; I needed the money to pay for my new car; but I also knew it was a small price to pay for the wonderful things God had in store for me.

5

The Lord Gives a Ministry

One evening I was invited to attend a Full Gospel Businessmen's Fellowship banquet to hear a Roman Catholic speaker. That evening I was asked to give a brief testimony of my own experiences since the baptism in the Holy Spirit. Then—of all things—they asked me to be their main speaker at the next month's meeting! In the enthusiasm of the moment and without giving it much thought, I agreed to come.

As I considered this engagement over the following weeks, I slowly began to panic. *Am I going to get up there and tell all about myself and about speaking in tongues and all these startling and wonderful things that have been happening to me? I made a mistake; I shouldn't have agreed to this foolish thing,* I pondered.

As the day approached, I was actually trying to devise a way of getting out of it, even to the point of saying I was sick. But I went. I could hardly eat, I was so frightened. *These people can teach me so much, and yet they want*

me to speak to them! Then the chapter president, Foley
Selvaggi, laid his hands on me and prayed. I stood up to
speak. After a word or two the Holy Spirit anointed me
with His power and I began to talk in a manner in which
I had never spoken in my life. At the conclusion of my
testimony I invited people to come forward to accept
Jesus Christ as Lord and Savior and be filled with the
Holy Spirit. I didn't plan to do that. I didn't even think
about it. I just did it.

All my life—even from childhood—I'd talk to people
about God and say all the proper religious things. After I
began seminary I'd speak of God as a clergyman is expected to speak. But nothing ever happened. Nobody was
ever changed—nor did they even care about what I was
saying even though they would politely listen.

That night, to my utter surprise, people came streaming
forward, many of them weeping, to receive Jesus Christ
and to be filled with the Holy Spirit. All I did was share
my experience with the Lord! And so I began to see with
my own eyes and in my own ministry the signs and wonders which Jesus promised would confirm the words of
His followers.

I continued to attend various prayer meetings and Bible
study groups all over the Pittsburgh area. At all these meetings I heard testimonies of how people had been healed by
the power of God. I even saw some of them receive their
healings.

And as I heard these exciting witnesses I began to sense
a growing desire within me that the Lord heal my eyes.
My eyes had caused so much heartache and retarded my
growth in so many ways. But as I pondered this thought,
another thought intruded: *Why be a spiritual hog, Mike?
You have a lot going for you. Your health is good. You
have a nice job. So many others in this world are a lot less
fortunate than you. Why want so much?"*

So I put it off, thinking that I shouldn't ask for healing

of my eyes. I allowed my actions to be guided by my thoughts and not by faith. A Presbyterian pastor whom I had known as a boy, the Reverend Dick Goodhart, was now pastor of a church in Pittsburgh. I discovered to my delight that Dick had also been baptized in the Holy Spirit. I decided that if I ever received prayer for my vision, I would ask him. I attended a prayer service at Dick's Eighth United Presbyterian Church just after having made this decision.

After the service I was introduced to a couple of his members, Bob and Jane Carter. Jane looked at me and asked abruptly, "Mike, what about those eyes of yours?"

I was stunned by her question. Who would dare ask such a question at first meeting?

"Would you like us to pray for your eyes?" Jane then added. I had no intention of asking for prayer but I could hardly avoid it now. Dick Goodhart then anointed me and the three of them prayed for my healing. I was crying while they prayed. I thought the Lord wouldn't heal my eyes because of all my past sins. Again, using my human logic, Satan stole my healing. I went out to the car and looked in the mirror. My eyes were still very crooked and I still couldn't see any better, so I put my glasses back on. And I sat there in the car, not healed. An unbelieving believer! I could believe Jesus Christ for salvation; I could believe Him for the baptism in the Holy Spirit; I could believe Him for someone else's healing; but I couldn't believe Him for *my* healing. I was an unbelieving believer.

When I spoke later at that first Full Gospel Businessmen's Fellowship banquet, I mentioned my eyes and asked everyone to pray for my sight. And they began to pray spontaneously as I was speaking. In fact, I had to stop speaking for a few moments while they were praying. I took off my glasses and finished the evening without them. I got into the car and looked in the mirror. The eyes were still very crooked and I still couldn't see any better.

"They're not healed," I said.

With my own lips I negated my healing. And I placed my glasses on my eyes again.

The following evening I attended a prayer service at St. Martin's Episcopal Church. This church is located along an interstate highway. On the roof of the church is a huge illuminated sign: JESUS IS ALIVE. Not only is that a sign on the roof, but it is a reality within. The congregation has been transformed by the power of the Holy Spirit. A boy stood up in St. Martin's prayer service to give a testimony. His name was Skip, and he reminded all of us who had been present at the previous week's prayer meeting how he had been coughing so badly at that earlier meeting. I recalled it vividly, because I had been speaking at that time, and Skip's interminable coughing had been so distracting. Immediately following that previous week's meeting Skip and his parents had come to me for prayer that Skip would be healed of this chronic asthma. Me? They wanted me to pray for his healing? I had never before laid hands on another person in order to pray for healing. But Skip had asked and I had prayed as he requested. So in this prayer meeting the following week, Skip stood up and told how God had healed him of asthma after Mike Gaydos prayed. I could hardly restrain my excitement. A deep thrill seemed to fill my being.

When the prayer meeting ended I went to the sanctuary and knelt. I asked Skip to pray for me this time. "Skip," I said, "we have to pray for something else in addition to my eyes. We have to pray about my pride and my vanity."

I was so self-conscious without my glasses because my eyes were extremely crooked. I had also just paid forty dollars for those glasses and I was afraid to lose my investment.

Skip asked God to heal my eyes. Then I said, "Skip, now I want you to take my glasses and place them on the altar. And pray that I won't take them back again."

Thirteen-year-old Skip took the glasses, carried them

up, and put them on the altar. Then he walked back very deliberately, placed his hands on my head, and prayed again.

"Your eyes are healed," came out so emphatically, so sincerely, that I believed in my heart the Lord really did something. His prayer had a quality which I knew reflected an anointing by the Spirit of God.

I drove home without my glasses. I didn't look in the rear-view mirror to examine my eyes, I just drove home. *I'll wait until I get home and by then they will be perfectly healed,* I thought. But I still had no depth perception, and I drove with some difficulty and when I arrived I looked in the mirror. My eye was still as crooked as ever. I covered my right eye and tried to see and I couldn't see a thing. "That eye isn't healed," I moaned, thinking of my glasses now sitting on St. Martin's altar.

Rather than reading the Word of God and praying and thanking and praising God in faith, I started grumbling and complaining. I had a "pity party" for myself at one A.M.

The next day I had to give a retreat, a day of renewal, at the parish where I was working. How could I possibly go down to St. Perpetua's Church the way I looked and feeling the way I felt? I didn't sleep all night as a result of worrying about my eyes. So in the morning—Sunday morning—I called Dick Goodhart at the Presbyterian Church and told him what had happened and asked what I should do.

"Mike," he said, "are you ready to pray?"

"Yes."

As Dick prayed over the phone I began to feel very much encouraged and more confident. I got dressed and went down to the parish.

Some high school students were standing in the parking lot. As I parked the car they walked up: "Father Mike, did you lose your glasses?"

"No."

"Did you break your glasses?"

"No."

"Did you get contact lenses?"

"No. The Lord healed my eyes."

I said it! That was my first positive affirmation of faith. And once I had said it, the assurance grew in my own spirit: "They *are* healed!" From that time on I confessed with my lips this statement of faith. As I spoke the word of faith, it came to pass. My sight improved. Daily I prayed much in the Spirit and spent much time reading the Scriptures, and I continued to see better and better—both eyes. I could cover the right eye and *see: After thirty years—I was seeing with my left eye!*

Occasionally I would feel a twinge in one eye or even in both. A quick look in the mirror would reveal that the eyes were less crossed. Often during a prayer service or a Bible teaching these twinges would occur. At times I could observe that my eyes were perfectly straight. Other times —usually when I was preparing to testify publicly—I would be standing in front of the mirror to comb my hair and notice that the left eye had wandered back toward its former abnormal position. I would be distressed momentarily, but I knew it was the devil trying to discourage me. I knew too that if the Enemy could defeat me in this area, he would defeat me in other areas also. So the healing continued, not steadily, but in successive instantaneous improvements which would occur without warning over a period of four or five weeks.

But not only physical sight improved. God gave me spiritual sight as well. I began seeing myself more and more as Jesus saw me. I began seeing others more and more as Jesus saw them. My self-centeredness was dropping away. The baptism in the Holy Spirit had already done so much for me, but I had not been allowing the Spirit to accomplish the greater liberating job He wished to do. Now I felt like praying for others. A new interest in the needs of other people was developing within me. I had eyes not only for myself but for others also. My lifelong mercurial personality—excited one week, depressed the next week—was stabilizing miraculously. Just one month after Skip placed my glasses on the altar, the Lord told me, as I sat in the Church of the Brethren where it all started, "Michael, stand and announce the good news. Tell these people that if they will take off their glasses on Christmas Day. . . ."

Although I had not yet realized it, the Holy Spirit had given me a ministry. How little I perceived what He had in mind!

I soon discovered that this ministry had a spontaneous quality; the Lord might manifest His gift at any time. Shortly after Christmas I attended the Pittsburgh Chapter banquet of the Full Gospel Businessmen. Many people whom I had never met were seated around me. As we ate dinner I began sharing what the Lord had done for me and for those on Christmas Day. On my right was a man named Bob Ashworth, an industrial designer at the United States Steel Research Laboratory. At the end of the speaker's message everyone stood. As we were worshiping the Lord, Bob turned to me and requested prayer for his eyes. Several of us laid our hands upon him and asked God to heal his vision. His eyes were both 20:200, very nearly what is considered to be "industrially blind," although his eyes were corrected with glasses to 20:20.

Bob dropped his glasses into my pocket. He got in his car but felt completely helpless behind the wheel, so his wife Betty had to drive home. Next morning Bob discovered that he could see surprisingly well: God's healing power had been working! He tried driving and had no difficulty, although that evening he noted that nighttime driving was still not easy. Bob realized also that his driver's license stated: "Corrective lenses required." So with disarming honesty he put an old pair of glasses in the car, and each time he drove Bob put them on. Sliding them down toward the end of his nose, Bob obediently watched the road while peering over the top of his glasses. A few weeks earlier his boss had been complaining about his own eyes. Bob had crawled out on a limb, suggesting that God could restore vision for both of them.

"Bob," replied his boss, "when you sit in that chair and read these papers to me without glasses, then I'll listen to you. Until then, I don't want to hear about your 'healing miracles!' "

Bob didn't say a word about his healing. He merely went to the lab the following Monday morning and deliberately read papers in front of his boss. With each day Bob's vision was improving. His supervisor stubbornly refused to comment. Bob was thoroughly enjoying the silent game, while the boss was obviously going through an intense struggle.

Finally a secretary blurted out, "Say, Bob, why aren't you wearing glasses any longer?"

The supervisor growled, "Oh, he's just trying to get me to go to church!"

After six weeks Bob received his required periodic physical examination. The company doctor was astonished! Without glasses, Bob's eyes were 20:70 and 20:50.

A few weeks later Bob went to his own Spirit-filled ophthalmologist, a physician who has confirmed many eye-healings. By now his eyes were 20:40 and 20:30. Today Bob still drives obediently with a pair of glasses resting on the end of his nose. He plans to go for a driver's examination as soon as the Holy Spirit completes His work.

Bob's observations about his eye-healing parallel my own. The Lord has been teaching him wonderful spiritual truths all the while the physical healing has been going on. Indeed, Jesus very definitely linked physical sight with spiritual sight after He healed the blind man outside the temple: "For judgment I came into this world, that those who do not see may see; and that those who see may become blind." (John 9:39)

Since Bob's healing, both his children have also received

eye-healings. One is already 20:20 and the other is very nearly there, as God's love continues to saturate the whole Ashworth family.

I began to realize that all I had to do was to tell publicly what God had done for my eyes. Faith would start building supernaturally in some of my listeners and their eyes were either greatly improved or totally healed. Actually, my own eyes, although the improvement was striking, were not completely healed yet. I still did not have central vision in the left eye and a slight crossing was still noticeable. No matter. God had already healed them when Jesus died on the cross; I believed that promise and testified repeatedly to it. The last symptoms would disappear as I continued to believe in my heart and affirm with my lips.

One Friday evening I attended a Jesus Rally sponsored by the Full Gospel Businessmen. One of the leaders asked me to give a brief testimony. So I told the young people how God had healed my eyes. Then I sat down and enjoyed the rest of the meeting.

Several months later a young man introduced himself to me. "Do you remember the Jesus Rally where you told of your eye-healing?" he asked.

"Well, as you spoke, God also spoke to me: 'Take off your glasses. I am healing you.'

"I tried, but there was no difference in my vision, so I continued wearing my glasses. All day Saturday He was repeatedly telling me, 'Take off your glasses.' But there was no difference, so I left them on.

"That night I couldn't sleep. The Holy Spirit was really working on me. Finally I challenged the Lord. 'All right, Jesus, if You are truly going to heal my eyes, then give me a sign that I should take off my glasses.' Then I went to sleep.

"The next morning I got up and turned on the television set. No particular station. As the picture came into focus, there *you* were, Father Mike. You! And you were telling on television how you had taken off your glasses and God had healed your eyes! I couldn't believe what I was seeing!

"I pulled off my glasses and the healing began. Today my eyes are normal. Praise the Lord!"

Since Christmas 1970, wherever I have testified—in living rooms, restaurants, campus meetings, churches, Full Gospel Businessmen's banquets—wherever I have had the privilege and joy of telling what Jesus has done for me— *something* wonderful happens. The message is so simple. It's the message of salvation through Jesus Christ and what He has done in the healing of my eyes. My message includes the utter failure of all my attempts to become good enough to make myself acceptable to God. Finally the revelation had come to me: Jesus—by His righteousness—makes me acceptable to God. So I speak the word of faith—God-given—and His Word does not return to Him void.

I began receiving invitations to speak in a number of churches. Some of the Protestant congregations in which I spoke were quite interested in hearing what the Holy Spirit was beginning to do among the Catholic Pentecostals. Many of them were frankly surprised as I was when I continued to go beyond my baptism in the Holy Spirit to tell of God's healing of eyes. It was not *my* healing that surprised them, but when various members of their churches began taking off their glasses and bubbling with delight—this was an unexpected variance from the usual order of worship.

I was trying all kinds of schemes to introduce the members of my family to Jesus and all that His Holy Spirit could do for them. Twice a year I have been taking my two nieces out to celebrate their birthdays. One of those birthdays was approaching. What an opportunity!

So I invited Ricki and Renee to spend a Sunday with me. We attended mass at St. Perpetua's Church, ate dinner in a restaurant, saw a stage presentation of Cinderella, got another snack, and then went to what I was interested in. We drove to the Church of the Brethren for their Sunday evening prayer service. *Perhaps God will use the girls to introduce my family to the work of the Holy Spirit,* I thought.

Ricki and Renee were captivated by the love and the joy manifested in the service. The three of us left the church, singing God's praises. While driving home we sang "Kum Ba Yah," and the three of us took turns making up a verse. "We love you, Lord," "We thank you, Lord," etc.

While we were riding along singing together, the thought occurred to me that the girls ought to be hungry. After all, if I had taken them out for the day, I didn't want them telling their parents that Uncle Mike brought them home hungry. Just then came Renee's turn to lead a verse. Her little voice sang out clearly, "We love Dairy Queen, Lord. . . ."

I could hardly get the car parked at the frozen custard stand which Renee knew was just ahead; I was almost doubled up with laughter. I tried to make a theological point of Jesus providing the answer to her prayer, but I don't know if it was very effective. The girls just continued licking their cones of frozen custard.

6

A Wave of Eye Healings

The May 1971 Greater Pittsburgh Charismatic Conference began with a testimony by a minister whose eyes
had been healed the year before. It was followed two days
later by the Reverend Bob Opie's testimony of receiving
his own eye healing just the previous night. Conference
Chairman Russ Bixler immediately seized the opportunity
and announced that Bob Opie and Michael Gaydos would
pray following the meeting for all who desired prayer for
their eyes. Russ commented later that he had never seen
such a crush of people attempting to get to Bob and me.
The Holy Spirit was anointing those meetings with great
power for healing and the people could sense it.

On the final evening of the Charismatic Conference,
Father Robert Arrowsmith, a Jesuit priest, gave an im-
pressive message on the Body of Christ. Again God spoke
to me as He had in December: "It is Christmas again.
Announce to the Body that the Lord will heal their eyes."

My reaction was similar to what I had experienced five

months before. "Lord, there are preachers and teachers and theologians from all over the world here. Do you really want me to give this message? If I am to speak, then you provide a place in the service."

I sat there feeling overwhelmed by the thought of interrupting this great service. My hands were perspiring, my throat was dry, and my heart was pounding. Finally there came a lull. I got to my feet and blurted it out. To my surprise it was no interruption, but was in perfect order and quite appropriate to the moment. A wave of thanksgiving swept the whole congregation. Here and there throughout the auditorium Christians heard the Word, received it, and acted upon it by taking off their glasses and removing their contact lenses. Some had their glasses back on before they left the conference, others replaced them within a day or two, some had to make appointments with their doctors for weaker prescriptions, but quite a few have never needed glasses since that evening. Later reports from a few who had attended the Conference indicated that in June another improvement in their eyes were noted and in July a further improvement.

Many Christians ask sincerely, "Why should there be only a partial healing? Can't God do the full work at one time?"

I don't know why, except that I think we have a clue in Mark 8:22–26. Jesus laid his hands upon a blind man, but instead of a complete healing, he could only "see men, for I am seeing them like trees, walking about." So Jesus laid His hands upon the man's eyes a second time and the healing was complete. This is the only biblical record of a need for a second healing, and I have often observed this same need for even a third and fourth "touch" before a person's eyes are fully healed by the power of God.

After the Charismatic Conference ended, two separate estimates of the number whose eyes God had either partially or totally healed agreed at "in excess of two hundred persons." And by the end of the summer enough testimonies had trickled in that we knew that Jesus had given his "second touch" to many of those partial healings. Especially thrilling was the repeated experience of watching young people, so troubled at the prospects of life-long partial blindness, (some with emotional problems quite similar to my own), delivered from that handicap. Such a glow appeared on their faces as they realized they had been released from this visual bondage as well as the social bondage!

On Friday evening I was helping to pray for the huge numbers of people who had responded to the invitation for individual ministry. I walked up to a young man and asked what I could do for him.

He introduced himself. "I'm Eldon Morehouse, pastor of the Union Grove Church of the Brethren near Muncie, Indiana. I recently received the baptism in the Holy Spirit, but I am having difficulty with the tongues. I would like the Lord to give me freedom in tongues and freedom to witness to my charismatic experience."

I placed my hands on him and prayed, mostly in tongues. Immediately Pastor Morehouse's voice was set free and he began to praise God in the Spirit quite fluently.

He returned to his church before Sunday and witnessed confidently from the pulpit to what God had been doing in his life. That initiated a steady flow of parishioners coming to him privately, requesting the baptism in the Holy Spirit for themselves.

About three weeks after the Conference Pastor Morehouse was driving his car out the driveway of his home. As he pulled the car onto the highway he happened to observe a mailbox about two-thirds of a mile down the flat Indiana road. As his eyes focused through glasses needed to correct a stigmatism and near-sightedness, the Lord spoke: "Take off your glasses!"

Without hesitation he removed the glasses and placed them on the seat beside him. Looking back promptly at the mailbox, he realized that he could see it as clearly without the glasses as he could with the glasses. "Thank you, Lord! But what does this mean?"

"Keep the glasses off and I will bless you!"

Pastor Morehouse is also a substitute school bus driver. Two months later he was required to undergo the annual physical examination for his license renewal. His doctor completed the medical certificate and gave it to his nurse. The nurse—who had heard the usual rumors about the "wild things" taking place at the Union Grove Church —said to Pastor Morehouse in front of the jammed waiting room, "Here is your certificate." Then, looking him straight in the eyes, she added in a determined tone, "You will note that it says, 'Glasses required.' "

He left the doctor's office in a quandary: "What do I do about that requirement now that my eyes are healed?"

He placed the certificate on a shelf in his living room, expecting to take it to the Bureau of Motor Vehicles for the eye test the following week.

The next week came, but the certificate could not be found. The whole family searched the house. It had simply disappeared. Pastor Morehouse had to pick up some printed materials in Muncie, so he decided to obtain another blank medical certificate at the Bureau of Motor Vehicles at the same time. He placed the blank certificate in his pocket and walked across the street to the print shop. There was their family doctor, also picking up a printing order. Pastor Morehouse seized the opportunity. "Doc, could you fill out another certificate for me? I've apparently lost the one you filled out before."

The doctor took out his pen and began to fill in the certificate from memory of the previous examination. Suddenly he stopped, looked up and asked, "How are your eyes?"

"Fine!" the pastor answered.

The doctor completed the form and signed it. A few days later Pastor Morehouse went to the Bureau of Motor

Vehicles to receive his license renewal. The officer tested his eyes and added to the certificate: "20:20."

Eight months later Pastor Morehouse found the lost prejudicial certificate. It had fallen behind the shelf and was wedged in a spot where it could not be seen!

He has never needed to wear glasses since that day when the Lord told him to keep them off. His eyes have continued to grow stronger. God has healed them so completely that today the other members of his family occasionally ask him to identify objects too distant for normal eyes to distinguish. His vision is now strikingly keen. And we had not even prayed for his physical eyesight!

All during the months since our prayer together, the Union Grove Church of the Brethren has been developing into a center of Christian ministry for the Muncie area. As their pastor's physical eyesight was being healed, his spiritual insight was also multiplying. Today his Indiana congregation is widely known for its effective ministry to persons in need. And their power continues to grow.

7

A New Direction

At the conclusion of the final service of the Charismatic Conference people continued to come to us for prayer, so that by the time midnight had passed Bob Opie and I were both utterly exhausted. When we had prayed for the last person I fell face-down on the hard floor and wept before the Lord. The empty auditorium echoed with my sobs. I cried because I was so aware of my own nothingness, my limitations, my past sins and shortcomings. I was so overwhelmed by the power, the love, the majesty, the goodness, and the mercy of God. I was awed by the beauty and the unity of the worship service we had so thoroughly enjoyed, and awed perhaps most of all by the signs and wonders Almighty God condescended to perform through us weak and frail humans. God is willing to use even me!

I just wanted to be alone. Other people were an intrusion into what had by now become my personal experience of worship. But my friends were becoming concerned for me. "Is Mike all right?" I could hear them asking one another.

"Oh, if I could just be alone!" I breathed quietly.

But several who loved me dearly crowded around, consoling me and praying for me. Joe and Chris Michalak insisted upon taking me home, but I resisted. I just wanted to stay in the chapel after everyone else had gone. Finally I agreed to let Joe and Chris follow me home in their car. The Michalaks are a precious Catholic Pentecostal couple who have been almost like second parents to me.

I pulled into our driveway and sat in the car. Joe and Chris drove in and parked behind me. "Lord! They're so good to me. But please!—make them go home."

Joe walked up to my car and comforted me in a fatherly way. He prayed gently with me and then drove away. I sat there for some time reveling in the Lord and all that He had done. He and I spent an intimately joyous time together in the car that night.

The next evening I was scheduled to speak at Calvary Temple in Washington, Pennsylvania. I entered the pulpit to read some Scripture and then began to tell of the charismatic renewal in the Roman Catholic Church. I had spoken only a few words before I began to weep again. The same sublime glory fell upon me, apparently just continuing from the night before. I tried reading the Scripture again. I began to pray aloud. But I simply could not go on. As I wept, the glory of God settled upon that worshiping congregation and the Lord ministered directly to His people that evening.

Whenever I would speak in a non-Catholic setting, such as a Protestant church or a prayer group composed largely of Protestants, quite often someone would challenge me before I left: "How can you say you are born again and baptized in the Holy Spirit and still remain a cleric in the Roman Catholic Church?" The challenger was usually a former Catholic.

Of course, these persons were sincere. But they left a Roman Church that had not yet experienced Vatican II, a Roman Church that had not even dreamed of a Pentecostal outpouring. Nevertheless, their challenging questions hurt. They would often back up their argument with allegations that were difficult to contradict.

I admitted that there were things wrong in the Roman Catholic Church; I admitted that I had been hurt by and disappointed in some persons in authority in the Church. But I always countered with the analogy noted earlier about my parents. I love my parents, but my love isn't blind to their faults. So it is with the Church. I found faults, but also many, many things that were good. And I knew it was ordained by God that I was to be a priest in the Roman Catholic Church. I responded politely to my challengers—again and again. These accusers displayed all aspects of Christianity except love; they were bitterly anti-Catholic.

But they left an increasingly uncomfortable feeling within me concerning my own church. One evening I was faced by a very determined former Catholic woman who simply could not comprehend the apparent contradiction of my baptism in the Holy Spirit and the Roman clerical garb I was wearing. She really put me in a turmoil. Yet that same evening God in His marvelous love placed me across the table from a precious, loving Pentecostal minister. He soberly told me of his own experience of receiving salvation and the baptism in the Holy Spirit forty years before. Because of this he was forced out of the Roman Catholic Church. There was still a wound in his spirit over that rejection. This pastor then listened to my story and gently encouraged me in what I was doing. The Church had hurt him deeply many years ago, but he spoke not one word to me against the Roman Catholic Church.

Russ and Norma Bixler were present at that meeting. They invited me to their home, although it was already quite late. Russ seemed to sense that something was bothering me. Over a cup of tea, he only had to ask a simple question to start my tears flowing. I fell apart. I cried and I cried, sobbing out the questions. "Am I really a Roman Catholic? How can I go on like this, with these contradictory feelings within me? Can I really blend the richness of my tradition with the liberty I have in the Holy Spirit? Where *do* I belong in the Body of Christ?"

Russ and Norma prayed with me. Then Russ confessed to his problems with his own denomination and told of the same difficulties being experienced by clergymen in *all* churches, whether Protestant or Catholic, liberal or fundamental, high church or low church, highly disciplined or independent. "Mike," he concluded, "denominational officials often react negatively to the Holy Spirit in *all* churches. God has placed you in the Roman Catholic Church. Has the Lord told you to leave your church?"

I emphatically responded through the tears, "No!"

"Well then, don't you ever leave the Roman Catholic Church!"

Everyone questions his denominational affiliation at some time. Some survive the questioning; some do not. I have had victory in this matter ever since that prayer over the cup of tea. I am thrilled to be a Roman Catholic cleric! To my delight I have discovered that even the "classic Pentecostals" are with few exceptions quite content to let me remain a Catholic. The Holy Spirit simply transcends those man-made divisions.

There are indeed prominent differences between denominations, but the Holy Spirit knows how to lead us to flow together, with Jesus Christ as the Head. Traditionally our Roman Catholic church and other liturgical churches have emphasized the Eucharist. Many Protestant denominations have centered upon the Word of God. Pentecostal churches are notable for walking in the power of the Holy Spirit. In my own life God has married all three emphases. I like to refer to my spiritual life as a three-legged milking stool. If you remove one leg the stool will collapse. For a balanced spiritual life all three are needed: first, communion, feasting at the Lord's table; second, Scripture, the Word of God; and third, the Holy Spirit, the very presence and power of God.

One of those whose eyes had been partially healed at Christmas time was Sister Kristin, of the Sisters of Charity. Her eyesight was extremely poor and could not be corrected to 20:20 even with the strongest glasses. Sister Kristin had been checked after Christmas by her ophthalmologist and he had noted a slight improvement. He changed her prescription. A month after her visit to the doctor she asked me to lay hands on her eyes and pray for healing. Within a few days her contact lenses began to irritate and her vision was cloudy.

Then—one at a time—she *lost* both contact lenses. That had never happened before. Sister Kristin needed prompt attention so the ophthalmologist gave her an early appointment. The improvement was startling! The doctor began checking his books for similar case histories. "We have records of eyes being slightly improved with contact lenses over a period of years," he said, "but your eyes, particularly the right eye, have improved more than any of my recorded cases in only one month! What are you doing?"

"I've had prayer for healing. God is doing it."

"Well, I don't understand it; but whatever your friends are doing for you, tell them to continue it." And once more he changed her prescription, which by now could correct her eyes to 20:20.

At the Charismatic Conference in May, the Reverend Bob Opie and I prayed for Sister Kristin again. And again God's healing power operated in her eyes. The only problem was new contact lenses, an expensive item. I prayed for her some months later, and her doctor was quite pleased to note another improvement. At the time of this writing Sister Kristin reports that her contact lenses are once more causing some irritation and her vision is cloudy again. Praise the Lord!

So many wonderful things are happening in my life, but there was some unfinished business remaining. I had not yet received my final ordination to the priesthood. I was still a seminarian. I had studies to complete. I wanted to return to seminary, but I wanted to experience all the power and love of the Holy Spirit in school too. I had to find such a seminary! I prayed, "Lord, now I want Your will to be done. If You want me to return to seminary to complete my studies for the priesthood, get me an invitation to attend a school where the Holy Spirit has His freedom."

I attended the monthly meeting of the Interfaith Ministers' Fellowship, a group of Spirit-filled clergymen of all denominations. Father Michael Scanlan, Rector (President) of St. Francis of Loretto Seminary, was present. After the meeting Father Scanlan asked me, "Mike, when are you going to finish seminary?"

I told him I didn't know when or where, to which he replied, "Well, I'd like very much to have you attend St. Francis of Loretto." Father Scanlan told of his desire that their seminarians be filled with the Holy Spirit and that they live and serve in His power.

I was excited once again about seminary! But I needed a bishop to sponsor me. I had left the Diocese of Steubenville, and now I was looking not only for such sponsorship for myself alone but also for sponsorship of my charismatic experience. Father Scanlan and I asked the Lord to reveal His will at this point. We agreed together in prayer that if it was God's will to return at this time to seminary, then He would lead a bishop to sponsor me.

Upon completion of my assignment at St. Perpetua's Church as Director of Religious Education, I was left with two free months, July and August. I wanted to do some traveling, combining a vacation with an opportunity to learn about the charismatic renewal in various parts of the nation. I had several invitations to speak in the South, so I packed my bags and left Pittsburgh. The speaking engagements were delightful. I found my life being enriched tremendously by the varying experiences and the interdenominational fellowship.

As the weeks passed, the two words "evangelist" and "evangelism" occasionally came to mind. These words occurred to me a number of times. Then one day I was visiting in a church when someone began to prophesy. The message was directed to me personally. I would be winning souls for the Lord, even on foreign soil. In another city the prophecy was repeated. Those who prophesied knew nothing about how the Lord had been dealing with my heart. And again came the same prophecy in yet a third city, of course through someone who knew nothing of the earlier message He had already placed within my own spirit.

My final destination on this trip was Melodyland Christian Center in Anaheim, California. I planned to be there for their Charismatic Clinic in August. The Reverend Russ Bixler had been invited to teach at the clinic, so I met the Bixler family in Kansas City and rode with them to Anaheim. As the clinic was beginning, Pastor Ralph Wilkerson recognized me in the congregation. He had been a teacher at the Pittsburgh Conference. Ralph invited me into the pulpit to speak briefly. "Brother Mike," he said, "would you be willing to pray with people during the clinic?"

I agreed and the Melodyland staff arranged for me to teach five sessions during the week. Suddenly I was teaching side-by-side with the very charismatic leaders whom I most wanted to teach me. I hurriedly shifted from the role of student to the role of teacher and back again all week. I needed to learn so much I didn't want to miss anything. At the same time God was healing eyes in each of my teaching sessions. Actually, it would hardly be said that I taught. I merely shared my testimony as usual and God's Holy

Spirit performed His loving work. How familiar to me the repeated message had become, yet how fresh and dynamic the Holy Spirit made it each time!

On that final day in the Charismatic Clinic a young third-grade school teacher named Lea was present. Lea had come from Bakersfield. She said to herself, "I'm tired of wearing glasses. I'll go hear Michael Gaydos speak."

Lea was walking around the corner of the building on her way to my class when a man walked up to her and said, "Lea, what can I do for you? I love you so much that if you ask anything in My name, I'll do it for you."

Lea was momentarily startled, yet completely at peace. It was Jesus. She couldn't see Him with her natural eyes, yet Lea insists that she could see Him. Jesus stood by her chair during the class, then told her, "Tell Brother Mike that as long as he glorifies Me in his meetings, these eye healings will continue."

During the class I said, "If you have taken your glasses off in faith, do not put them on again." Lea had already put her glasses in her purse.

She walked out determined not to tell anyone about her visitation. A moment later her girl friend Ruth greeted her and Lea burst into tears. Ruth asked, "Did you see Jesus?"

"Yes!"

So Lea returned immediately to the classroom to tell me what the Lord had said. She cried for half an hour. After she regained her composure, Lea went to her car and drove to her room in Long Beach without using glasses. She could read every sign along the road!

One week later Lea lost her healing. All the symptoms returned, yet she didn't lose her faith. Lea was puzzled, bewildered, and disappointed, but she was also very persistent. She *knew* that Jesus had healed her.

Lea taught school for six weeks, stubbornly refusing to wear her glasses. Much that she needed to read she couldn't see. Her effectiveness as a teacher was severely limited. Even then she would not replace the glasses on her eyes. During those six difficult weeks God was healing her emotional problems. Spiritually she was growing by leaps and bounds. One night in October Lea knelt before the Lord and forgave the one person toward whom she had felt great bitterness for a number of years. She cried and cried. And Lea got up from her knees with eyes that were healed permanently. Today they remain 20:20.

I have never forgotten what Jesus told me through Lea. Praising Him is so ordinary and spontaneous in my private devotional life; I merely do the same in public too. A Catholic friend in Anaheim pointed out a perceptive observation. He noted that most of the healings that took place in my classes occurred during or following singing in the Spirit—which is pure praise. The Holy Spirit simply responds whenever we praise Jesus.

The Charismatic Clinic in Anaheim was so exciting. Person after person reported that Jesus had healed his eyes. And I was learning so much at the same time. Each day's class would bring at least one pastor to invite me to speak in his church. By the end of the week I had received invitations to speak all over California!

I started up the coast, speaking first in a Roman Catholic Church, then a Pentecostal Church, then a Presbyterian Church—such a delightful variety! I walked into a church in Redwood City one hour before the service was scheduled to begin. The church was jammed with young people, all of them praying and worshiping the Lord. I examined my watch—perhaps it had stopped. But the pastor told me this was customary. So many of them had been hippies, social rejects, drug addicts. Now they were well-dressed and clean and excited about Jesus. The service began on time, but it was actually a continuation of what had already been going on. The worship and prayer continued for an additional hour.

Then I stood to give my testimony. There seemed to be no sense of surprise at my story; the usual astonished delight was missing. Those young people had no difficulty believing anything I said because they had already experienced the miraculous saving and cleansing grace of Jesus Christ. A number of them had been set free from worse bondage than I had ever known. When I finished my message everyone stood for more prayer and praise. As we all ministered to the Lord, He ministered healing to the congregation. Spontaneously the young people began removing their glasses and walking to the front. Orderly and confidently they filed out of their seats. Only the Holy Spirit told them what to do. They quietly placed their glasses on the little altar. By the time the young people reached their seats again, a number of them could read their song sheets. Some delightedly opened their Bibles to soak up the Scriptures without artificial assistance. The pile of discarded glasses and contact lenses must have cost originally several thousand dollars.

Not all were healed at one moment. Several had to remove their glasses before coming down the aisles—they were already causing headaches. Others groped for the front—and were healed while returning to their seats. Still others observed partial healings and more woke up seeing clearly the next morning. As always, there were some who didn't dare step out in faith, along with those who had timidly removed their glasses, squinted a little and then replaced them comfortably over their eyes.

Several days later we left for Pittsburgh. As for me, I was to return to seminary. I headed for home with my mind prepared to complete my studies for final ordination to the priesthood, yet with my spirit feeling a call into full-time evangelism. I could not forget those three prophecies!

So as a final test for resolving the matter one way or the other, I prayed, "Lord, if you want me to be an evangelist rather than a seminary student for this school year, then I ask you now to provide Father Scanlan's approval and blessing."

As soon as we arrived in Pittsburgh I called Father

Scanlan, telling him about all the exciting things God had been doing. He reacted immediately: "Mike, this would be a tremendous opportunity—not only to give but also to learn! There is much you can learn by being out serving that cannot be found in the classroom. We would be withholding your needed ministry if you attended seminary this year. Besides, as of this time no bishop has offered to sponsor you."

8

Catholic Evangelist

There it was. With Father Scanlan's enthusiastic blessing, I stepped out on faith and headed for eastern Pennsylvania. I wanted to attend the regional convention of the
Full Gospel Businessmen's Fellowship. I was so hungry to
learn all I could.

As a youngster I used to play a game called "Mother,
may I?" I would ask such questions as "Mother, may I
take a baby step?" "Mother, may I take a kangaroo step?"
and "Mother, may I take a giant step?"

For thirty years all I had ever done was take baby steps
of faith. With the baptism in the Holy Spirit the Lord
began to create opportunities for giant steps of faith. It
was a giant step to leave my glasses on the altar of St.
Martin's Episcopal Church. Another opportunity for a
giant step developed when I set out on a year of evangelism, not knowing where I was going or what was to
happen.

I had purchased a new Mustang to commute to my

teaching positions at the business college and St. Perpetua's Church. Now I was leaving Pittsburgh and I wouldn't need the car. It seemed appropriate to give the Mustang to my parents in partial repayment of my years of wearing out their cars. My first car—and just a year later I was giving it away—it was hard to believe. So they sold their old car and accepted mine.

I arrived at the motel where the convention was being held. As I closed the door of the motel room, it all hit me. A full year of evangelism—and I hadn't even one speaking engagement. Where will I go? What will I do? How about money? I had only the cash in my pocket. I knew my parents would stand behind me if I had financial needs, but I already looked rather foolish in their eyes. I felt so alone! I didn't even have a car. The tears began to flow. I was frightened and excited at the same time. I had done many foolish things in my life, but this was surely the most foolish—and yet I felt quite confident. The flesh was at war with the spirit!

I was quietly crying alone, my brain overwhelmed with those conflicting thoughts, when the telephone rang. It was Pastor Ralph Wilkerson from Anaheim, California: "Hi, Mike. How are you doing?"

"Fine!" I assured him as I wiped my wet cheeks and tried to calm my distressed heart.

"I've been trying to locate you. It has taken quite a number of phone calls. I understand you didn't return to seminary."

"That's correct."

"Well, a team of ministers from Melodyland and other churches are going to Mexico to hold a Charismatic Clinic in November. We would love to have you come along to share as a part of the team. We'll pay all your expenses. Would you be willing to take part?"

"Praise the Lord! I'd be glad to come!"

"You can also speak here at Melodyland again before

we all leave for Mexico. We'll expect you in November."

I hung up the telephone. I was stunned. "Thank you, Jesus!" The Lord didn't merely confirm my leap of faith into evangelism, he sent fireworks, flares, and flashing lights to underscore the message. With the joy of this confirmation exploding in my heart, I changed clothes and bounced into the opening session of the convention.

Immediately I was recognized by some who had attended the Greater Pittsburgh Charismatic Conference in May. They asked me to share a short testimony during the meeting. I told briefly what God had done in my life, read some Scripture, and led several of my favorite choruses. Again the anointing of the Lord fell upon the service as He healed eyes here and there throughout the meeting hall.

Before the Convention ended I received a number of invitations from pastors to speak in churches in New York, New Jersey, and Washington, D.C. Each engagement would lead to another invitation, filling the entire two-and-a-half months from September until Thanksgiving. At every service the Lord was faithful. People accepted Jesus Christ, were filled with the Holy Spirit, or received healing for their eyes. How exciting to have Him bless me while He was blessing thousands of others!

After Thanksgiving with my family, I flew to Los Angeles, preached at Melodyland, and left for the Mexican Charismatic Clinic with the team. The primary purpose was to introduce the charismatic renewal to Mexico. The Clinic in Mexico City was held at the Roman Catholic Seminary of the Holy Spirit. *How appropriate!* I thought.

Because I was the only Roman Catholic cleric on the team, everyone felt it would be good if I gave the opening message. As I walked into the first evening's service I was introduced to a woman who was wearing a collar brace. She told me it was a traction device and she would have to wear it the rest of her life. By suffering like this she was entering into the passion—the suffering and the crucifixion—and thereby becoming ever closer to and more like Jesus. This was what she believed.

I admired her courage and her willingness to suffer for Jesus, but I challenged her with the promises of God. I read her some verses of Scripture which told how Jesus shed His blood that our sins might be forgiven; how Jesus by His sufferings bore our infirmities, our sorrows, our sicknesses, our diseases; how Jesus demonstrated the will of God that we be whole in body, mind, and spirit. I told her if there is to be suffering it ought to be for the gospel's sake. Suffering should come upon the Christian only in the form of persecution for Jesus Christ. Then I asked her, "Would you begin believing with me right now that before this service is over God will heal you completely?" She cautiously agreed.

With that I went to the sanctuary to speak. Among other things I taught several choruses which included the raising of hands. I could see this same woman, and she was obviously unable to lift her hands because of the severe pain. I gave my own testimony, preached and proclaimed the Word of God on faith and healing. At the close of my message we all again praised the Lord in song. The woman with her neck in the collar brace began to lift her hands with the rest of us. Tears of joy—not pain— came streaming down her cheeks. The Lord had healed her as His Word was going forth. Everyone saw what had happened and rejoiced with her.

This one miracle alone opened the door. The Mexican people who attended the Clinic were ready to receive the full gospel message of salvation in Jesus Christ, the baptism in the Holy Spirit, and the healing power of the Lord. It was a glorious clinic. A new day for the gospel is dawning in Mexico.

I had been apprehensive about the necessity of speaking through a Spanish interpreter. *How can I with my spontaneous style of speaking possibly work with an in-*

terpreter? I thought. But I discovered that the Holy Spirit bridges that language barrier beautifully. In spite of my lifelong difficulties with languages, I found myself singing Spanish songs of praise within moments of first hearing them! The Spirit-filled interpreter and I each seemed to sense immediately what the other was doing.

I remained at the Seminary of the Holy Spirit for an additional week after the clinic ended. This was a delightful experience, recalling all the good memories of my own seminary days. I could attend mass every day, walk quietly through the gardens, and share individually with hungry seminarians. They delightedly taught me Spanish expressions, we ministered to the poor together and particularly to the nuns who worked among the poverty-stricken. The seminarians also bicycled with me through Mexico City, showing me many of the famous old missions. I returned to Anaheim refreshed and renewed.

Testimonies of eye-healings continued to follow my ministry. I had been at Melodyland only a brief time in November before we left for Mexico. While I was speaking there in Anaheim a woman named Ruth had claimed healing for her eyes. Later she told how she had felt strangely different. However, Ruth continued to wear her glasses and thought little about it after the service.

A couple of weeks later Ruth went to get her driver's license. She had just moved to Cypress, California, from Texas. The police officer asked her to remove her glasses in order to take the eye test. She protested that she couldn't see clearly without them and that her Texas license stated, "Corrective lenses required."

"Take them off!" he responded firmly.

The officer tested her eyes and stated flatly, "You don't need glasses to drive."

"Do you really mean it?"

"Yes, you don't need glasses to drive. You can see quite well at a distance."

Ruth discovered that she did still need bifocals for

reading, yet her eyes have continued to improve since then and are today almost completely normal. Through these months since November 1971, Ruth has spent many hours in Bible study. She also reports the same additional testimony that so many others tell. While God is healing their physical eyes He is also giving them precious spiritual revelations as well. "Eyes to behold Him" indeed!

I left Anaheim to speak in other churches as invitations continued to flow. One of these churches had a large cassette tape library. I asked if I might borrow some and listen to them in my motel room. On one tape the speaker was dealing with the subject of restitution and reconciliation. As I listened, the Holy Spirit began to remind me of that very foolish thing I had done in high school. I liked the men's clothing I was selling at my part-time job. I liked stylish clothing too much: when my money was exhausted I took the clothes I wanted plus cash from the register. As I listened further, the Lord by His Spirit told me to write a letter to Allen Lebovitz, confessing my sin and asking his forgiveness.

I had confessed the sin to God and asked *His* forgiveness years before. But now the Lord was instructing me to confess to Mr. Lebovitz. Not only that, He also said to include a check to cover the cash and merchandise stolen.

"Lord! I can't do that! I'm a cleric! What will this man think of me if I write such a letter? I just can't do it!"

The tape wound on and on. "Please, Lord!" I begged as the Holy Spirit "twisted the knife" in my spirit.

"For the word of God is living and active and sharper than any two-edged sword, and piercing as far as the division of soul and spirit." (Hebrews 4:12)

"All right, Lord. I'll do it'!" I agonized my way to a commitment.

The stationery was quite handy and my checkbook was just as accessible. "Tomorrow," I thought. "Sure, I'll do it tomorrow after I've had a chance to think about what to say to Mr. Lebovitz."

Still I procrastinated, with one delaying excuse after another. Suddenly I hit upon an idea that gave me the first comfort I'd had over the matter.

"Lord, if You really want me to write that letter, then You provide a sign. Provide some confirmation that this is what You want me to do." And I breathed more easily.

A few days later I was speaking at a conference at Springs of Living Water, a large retreat home in northern California. During the second day of the conference I was eating lunch with a young man. I asked him what he enjoyed doing in addition to serving the Lord.

He replied, "Oh, I love to play the guitar."

"Well, why haven't you been bringing your guitar to the meetings?"

"Brother Mike," he answered with heaviness in his voice, "before I knew the Lord I played in a rock band. We got all our equipment by stealing it. I have a very expensive electric guitar—worth about five hundred dollars. I stole it too. Every time I begin to praise the Lord on that guitar, He says, 'Don't praise Me on that stolen guitar!' "

The young man continued by telling that the Lord had spoken to him three times about returning the guitar. Each time the Holy Spirit convicted him, he returned it to the store where he had stolen it, and each time he would "chicken out" almost at the door.

Suddenly he stopped and asked, "Brother Mike! What's wrong?"

I was as pale as I could be. "The Lord is speaking to me through you," I said.

Then I told him about my own thefts from the clothing store and about the Lord's dealing with me just a few days before.

By this time we had both lost our appetites. We left the table and entered the chapel. I knelt and he prayed for me. Then he knelt and I prayed for him.

At this point I should have run straight to my room,

written a letter and a check and mailed them immediately. But I delayed again. "I've got to do it!" I resolved. Yet I didn't. The agony was intense.

A few days later I was reading a book. The author—and I should have anticipated it—got to the subject of confession and restitution.

"Okay, Lord! You're coming through loud and clear."

This time I sat down and wrote the letter. I estimated the value of what I had stolen and wrote a check. And I mailed it!

The letter served a fourfold purpose. First, confession—God expects us to confess our sins to Him and to those whom we have wronged. Second, restitution—He wants us to restore whatever things possible. Third, reconciliation—God desires that we do what is needed to reconcile ourselves to those we have wronged. And fourth, witness—I witnessed to Mr. Lebovitz about the Lord Jesus Christ, telling how it was He who was straightening out my life. Jesus emphatically declared in John 15 that He expects us to bring forth fruit, and He will sometimes "prune" us that we may bring forth more fruit.

That letter was one of the most difficult things I have ever done in my life. Yet it provided one of my greatest opportunities for growth. It was an exercise of my own will in surrendering to the lordship of Jesus Christ. I was free from another burden which had been limiting my life.

Some Christians assume that all clergymen are sinless. When I played priest as a child, everyone thought I was angelic. Repeatedly friends and relatives spoke of me in these terms. Teachers never suspected that I would cheat on a test, as I did several times. Mr. Lebovitz accepted my honesty without question. After all, I *was* the Michael Gaydos who was going to be a priest!

One of my pleasant associations there at Springs of Living Water was a sweet, loving young man named Michael Munger. I was so impressed by Michael's sincere love for the Lord and by his gentle personality. After some time together he casually handed me a tract and said, "You may enjoy reading my story."

What a shock to read Michael's testimony! This gentle Christian was a convicted murderer of his own father! He had been thoroughly immersed in the San Francisco drug culture, as well as witchcraft and various forms of oriental religion. How I praised God as I looked from the tract to Michael and back again! Jesus had completely transformed a hate-filled murderer. "The old things passed away; behold, new things have come. Now all these things are from God." (2 Corinthians 5:17b,18a)

I have heard "man" described in many ways. One of my favorite descriptions is that "Man is an incarnate question mark"—a question mark in the flesh. We ourselves may be our own greatest mystery. One day we get out of bed and do something extremely good, beautiful, or noble. At the end of the day we reflect: "I never realized I was capable of reaching such heights of goodness." Yet another day we get out of bed only to perform an act so low, so despicable, so sinful, that we ponder it too: "I never realized I was capable of sinking to such depths of degradation." A question mark in the flesh!

A social scientist says, "Tell me what books a man reads and I'll tell you who he is." A psychologist says, "Tell me what a man thinks when he is alone and I'll tell you who he is." A philosopher says, "Tell me who a man's friends are and I'll tell you who he is." Another says, "Tell me where a man spends his money, on what he places value, and I'll tell you who he is." Yet I am convinced that all these criteria would give only a partial picture. After my own limited number of years of experience in study, in education, in camp counseling, in evangelism, I am convinced that if you will describe to me a man's relationship to Jesus Christ, I can tell you who he is.

When a man has a direct encounter with the living Jesus Christ and responds by surrender, repentance, and thanksgiving, he is no longer an incarnate question mark, going about searching, questioning, craving, wishing. When that man further submits himself to being baptized in the Holy Spirit and lifts his hands in worship in other tongues, praising God in spirit and truth, he becomes an emphatic exclamation mark! He is a man who has discovered who he is, and more important still, he himself has been *discovered*. He knows what life is all about; he knows life's meaning and purpose.

For so many years, although I knew Jesus, I didn't recognize my need for a Savior. I was busy trying to save myself. *I* was making the effort to be holy. Now I know that holiness is not the way to Jesus, but rather Jesus is the way to holiness. For many years I didn't realize my need for a Lord. I was busy being my own lord. I mapped out all my own plans. I merely asked God to endorse and bless those plans. How much simpler and more joyous it is now that *Jesus* makes me holy and *Jesus* plans my schedule. I know He has a beautiful plan for my whole life, and I am bubbling with the anticipation of watching Him unfold this exciting future.

It was an exciting year of evangelism, a year of witnessing to what the Lord could do when a frightened seminarian gave Him the year He asked for. Before Christmas the entire year was nearly filled in my datebook. God led me through much of the United States, including Hawaii —to Mexico, Italy, Greece, and the Holy Land. Everywhere I was able to share my testimony and proclaim the Word of God concerning the faith and healing. And everywhere nominal Christians of all denominations—especially Roman Catholics—were introduced to Jesus Christ, filled with the Holy Spirit, or healed. Of course, eye-healings predominated at all the services.

During that winter of 1971–72 His scheduling made possible one of the greatest thrills of my life—a visit to the Holy Land. It was all enjoyable, but the highlight for me was entering the garden tomb. As our group huddled together in and about this grave where one tradition says that Jesus was laid, we all began to realize about the same time the fact that no physical tomb could hold Jesus. He's alive! We burst spontaneously into a song of praise: "Alleluia!" The Holy Spirit's anointing fell upon us. His joy bubbled and the tears flowed. He is truly risen, and He reigns!

We returned to California and I resumed the schedule God had arranged, traveling from one church or prayer group to the next. At Bishop, California, I skied all day and preached in the evening. That was a most difficult week of evangelism—such fun! The Sierras were fabulous! Riding the ski lift provided some humorous opportunities to witness for the Lord. Steve and I were riding up together, praising the Lord in song, while the woman in the chair ahead of us made an obvious show of disdain over the two "nuts" in the chair behind her. On the way back down the slope, we had the delightfully ironic opportunity to pull her out of a snowdrift.

But the times I rode the double chair with a stranger were really something! "Where are you from?" they would invariably ask on the fifteen-minute ride.

"From Pennsylvania."

"From Pennsylvania! And you come all the way out here to ski?"

"No. I'm a Catholic, and I'm in California as an evangelist."

"A Catholic evangelist?"

And so the door would be opened once more to tell of Jesus and His saving, healing power. So captive an audience is not easy to find. Ride after ride provided delightful opportunities and occasional hungry hearts.

So many Americans think it strange that I should be a Roman Catholic evangelist. Actually, the Roman Church has *always* been evangelistic. I am merely one in a significant historical line of Catholic evangelists. But the novelty to the person who is unaware of this tradition is so striking that it never fails to provide another tailor-made chance to witness.

When we flew to Mexico City Ralph Wilkerson, Michael Esses, Dick Mills, and I were seated side-by-side in the plane. We were laughing and praising the Lord together. Most passengers nearby were trying to get happy on other spirits. A stewardess stopped to inquire why we were so happy. So we introduced ourselves—two Protestant ministers, a Roman Catholic cleric, and a Jewish rabbi —and told her that we were on an evangelistic team. The stewardess' astonishment could not be hidden, and the four of us enjoyed the additional delight of seeing that revelation reflected in her face.

9

Hawaii

In early spring 1972 the Lord arranged my schedule to include Hawaii. Excitedly I flew to the Islands to witness to several Full Gospel Businessmen's chapters. At the first breakfast meeting I was sitting there listening to myself being introduced, enthralled by the beauty of the surrounding land and sea. I was so delighted by the thrill of at last being in Hawaii. Then I stood up to speak and two lovely ladies put a flower lei around my neck and kissed me on each cheek.

I was speechless. Finally I grinned and blurted out, "If my bishop could only see me now!"

The meeting erupted with laughter. Such a happy welcome to the Islands! The visitor is always greeted with the lei, and if he intends to return he throws the lei into the ocean as he is leaving. I spent more than two weeks in Hawaii, first on the Island of Hilo and then on Oahu. While I was in Hawaii the Roman Catholic prayer group at Chaminade College of Honolulu asked me to share with them also. Father Gary Colton of St. John Vianney Church —that name brought back memories—was the director of the prayer group. This particular community was a special blessing to me.

In 1970 Father Gary and Sister Irene Solzbacher and some high school students heard a tape by Kevin Ranaghan. Through Kevin's testimony tape several received the baptism in the Holy Spirit and a prayer community began to grow. Two years later I was invited to speak to the group, which by now had grown to the size where they had to forsake the classroom and use the chapel. More than 250 attended the mass we celebrated and remained to hear my testimony. The spirit of this prayer community was altogether lovely. Father Gary reports that his bishop has questioned him with enthusiasm concerning the Pentecostal outpouring and has further expressed a desire to appoint Father Gary as chaplain of the Pentecostal community. The bishop has requested and received periodic reports on the mushrooming Catholic charismatic movement in the Islands. Every week, nominal Roman Catholics are receiving Jesus Christ as Lord, then moving into the baptism in the Holy Spirit. A genuine revival is also occurring in Father Gary's St. John Vianney Church in Kailua as many laymen are reaching out through several home prayer meetings also.

For ten exciting days at Easter time I was ushered from prayer group to church to prayer group. At each place we told about the community at Chaminade College, and it began to mushroom in size again. The Chaminade group has become a center for ministry in Honolulu, even somewhat of a model for conducting prayer meetings.

On Saturday before Easter I spoke to the Honolulu chapter of the Full Gospel Businessmen. Sister Irene, one of the founders of the Chaminade prayer group, was present. Her own personal experiences I knew were rather dramatic, so several months later I asked Sister Irene to relate her testimony. I hardly realized how much God meant to her!

"The Charismatic renewal has been a real turning point in my life," she told me. As Sister Irene related her life story I was impressed with some of the similarities to my own experience with God. "I remember when I was only two years old I had a sudden awareness of God's love, and that realization literally overwhelmed me even at that young age. As a child growing up in Europe during World War II, God was quite close to me, as He was to our whole family. Being refugees, we knew the experience of God's deliverance many times. He always seemed so close to me that I just could *not* be aware of how wonderful He is.

"We came to the United States when I was seven. I had long since known that the Lord wanted me to be a sister. Furthermore, if that was what He wanted, it was what I wanted too. When I was eight, He let me know that I was to be at Maryknoll; He wanted me to be a missionary.

"I entered Maryknoll at the age of 19, having benefited from a wonderful pastor during my teen years who believed everybody should have a deep relationship with Christ. At Maryknoll however, I began to doubt my earlier experiences, and God did not seem close to me anymore. The convent was not conducive to spirituality. I was now interpreting my high moments with God as simple emotion. We had so many prayers to say that I didn't have time to pray. I was almost fighting God. At that time the Maryknoll spiritual discipline was thought to be correct, but—Praise the Lord!—we have now changed and we all have more freedom to pray and worship as the Spirit leads.

"Two years ago I was becoming almost desperate. I wondered if I needed psychiatric help. My frustrations at trying to pray made me feel as if I were hitting my head against a stone wall. Having known what prayer could be only heightened the agony.

"Then, when a friend shared his charismatic experience

at our home, I knew instantly that this was what I was looking for. I wanted what he had, and I wanted it very badly. Three days later several of us gathered to pray. Immediately I sensed that familiar nearness of God I had known before. Two weeks later I received the baptism in the Holy Spirit. Now I know why some thought the apostles were drunk at Pentecost. Everybody thought I was drunk too.

"This experience changed my life in many ways. Prayer became so simple. Christ's presence was so real that I couldn't miss Him; I didn't need to resurrect an old memory. Through His Spirit He began speaking to me as clearly as the person standing next to me. *He* was now directing my actions. Christ would tell me to go somewhere and I went, not knowing why. But when I arrived, I would always find someone in need. In counseling people, I would on occasion discover myself saying things without logical explanation only to find that it made quite good sense in the end.

"I have always been impetuous, and I put up a front of being happy-go-lucky. But underneath I was often anxious and fearful. The Lord removed the anxiety and the fear. For the first time I felt truly free. No longer did I need to hide my feelings. The whole world could witness what was going on inside me and I didn't care. This freedom was tremendous. The sheer joy of not putting up an artificial mask was thrilling. This joy was real now. Two years later that same joy still remains with me.

"When I heard you were coming, Mike, I had a sense that the Lord was going to do something. I jokingly said to Father Gary, 'Here go our glasses!' When you spoke at the Full Gospel Businessmen's Breakfast that Saturday morning, the Lord really worked powerfully in me. I knew He was asking me to step out on faith to do something that would be quite difficult.

"From the time I was in seventh grade I haven't been able to see the blackboard. For a time I memorized the eye chart in order not to wear glasses. But within another year or so I was not only unable to read the chart, I couldn't even find it! My eyes continued to grow worse until the right eye was 20:300 and the left eye 20:500. They remained much the same until now—at the age of thirty-eight—my eyes suddenly changed that Saturday morning. But I was terrified at the thought of giving up my glasses. As others prayed for me, I received courage enough to give the glasses to someone. I actually drove home without them. I could feel my eyes growing stronger that morning.

"I am a medical student—now, at my age—and we students had been practicing giving each other physical examinations. Every week my eyes had been tested with the near-vision chart, the kind you hold only fourteen inches away from your eyes. During our practice examinations, my near vision had consistently checked 20:200 in the right eye and 20:400 in the left eye. After I returned home that morning I carefully checked again. To my joy I found the right eye 20:40 and the left eye 20:70! The next day the right eye was 20:20 and the left eye 20:50. They have remained the same during the months since.

"The distant vision however did not improve at that time. Although I can read all day without glasses and without a resultant headache—strangely enough I could see no better at a distance. At your encouragement, Mike, I went to the Clinic to try to have 'Corrective lenses required' removed from my driver's license. Again the near vision checked good, but the distant vision was no better. The doctor asked why I thought my vision should be improved.

"I explained what had happened, and he looked rather bemused. Unable to explain why the near vision had improved so suddenly, he observed that the distant vision was 'an impossible situation.' It would require a change in the shape of the eyeball.

"In a moment I understood. Now my medical record was in black and white. When the distant vision clears up,

God will receive all the glory. For I *know* He has healed my eyes! Changing the shape of my eyeball would be a simple task for the Lord.

"Throughout these several months God has been giving me—as you said He would—increased spiritual vision. I plan to be a psychiatrist. It seems almost a miracle that God has opened every door to get me into medical school at my age, but here I am—the 'senior citizen' of the medical school. The Lord is using me in a ministry of counseling right in the school. And I sense His leading me in the direction of unifying psychiatric methods and the spiritual means that God uses to accomplish His work. I also feel that He wants me to work with addicts, alcoholics, emotionally disturbed persons. The *real* poor—the weak, the hopeless, the confused, the frustrated, the anxious, the unhappy—are those for whom God has a special love. The Church as I see it is not a Church of the strong, but the Church of the weak. I so enjoy going to the State Institution for the Retarded to help with the services and to witness how those with such special human handicaps are able to receive great blessings from the Lord. Speaking and praying before groups used to be quite difficult before He turned my life right-side-up. Now I merely pray, and God gives me just the words to say which will speak to the needs of the hearers.

"I feel so blessed in being in the positive atmosphere of acceptance here in the Medical School. I have met very little sarcasm and very little resistance when I insist that the Lord can work in healing. There is a respect for Christian principles among my associates. I can be myself freely and can share my faith without restrictions. I am so grateful to God for this.

"So often He makes me aware of my limitations, my failures. Then—in my weakness—He helps people through me to find peace and understanding and acceptance and joy. The Lord is drawing so many of those 'really poor' to our prayer groups. It is so exciting and so rewarding to see His healing power go forth to enrich such poverty-stricken lives. How I appreciate His inviting me to share a part in these experiences of His love! Spiritual sight and physical sight certainly have grown together in my life."

Sister Irene's recent life in the Spirit underscores a scripture verse I love to quote. John 20:20 is the basis for genuine 20:20 vision. "The disciples therefore rejoiced when they saw the Lord." God gives more than physical vision. He wants us to see lots more than a world of people and books and flowers and trees. He wants us to see the Lord Jesus Christ, who poured out His own blood to redeem that world from sin and sickness and death. Indeed, all genuine modern disciples are glad when they see the Lord.

Many who have prayed that their eyes be healed wonder why nothing has happened. And I have wondered too: does our capacity to receive God's healing for physical eyesight depend upon our willingness to grow in spiritual eyesight? I am thoroughly persuaded that God wants to heal everyone's eyes. In fact, He doesn't want our eyes ever to be less than perfect. I know this is His will, for Jesus clearly demonstrated that divine will by healing *all* the blind who came to Him when He walked this earth. But—to repeat the question—do we block God's healing power for our physical blindness by an unwillingness to give up some of our *spiritual* blindness? Because I see the two healings—physical and spiritual—going hand-in-hand and because I am so convinced that God desires to heal our eyes more than we want to be healed—well, I am pondering the matter.

"Jungle bunnies!" That's what they called the youthful "hippies" from the Mainland. Jungle bunnies are young people, alienated from society, family, and church. They have retreated into the jungles of Hawaii to escape what they consider a phony world. They live communally—and naked—amid quite primitive conditions. One aspect of their existence is not so primitive however; they seem to have located a continuing source of modern drugs. They live largely off the jungle and some crops they plant themselves. The jungle bunnies are completely immersed in the occult—worshiping the sun, practicing meditation and various forms of oriental religion.

I spent some time at a Christian commune where the young people were building a store. Ken, the elder of the commune, was driving their jeep when he saw a girl walking toward town. He stopped and gave her a ride. She was a jungle bunny—on her way to buy some of the few civilized supplies they use. Ken talked to her about Jesus and she agreed to visit their commune. There she accepted the Lord, received prayer to clean herself of all the demonic filth in which she had been immersed, then stayed some days to study the Bible with the young Christians.

Later Ken and I took her back to the jungle in the jeep. While she was picking up her few belongings and collecting all her occult literature and objects to burn later, she witnessed to the others about Jesus. Ken suggested that *our* best witness would be to use the jeep to pull tree stumps out of a newly-cleared field the jungle bunnies planned to cultivate. So we went to work. With the jeep it was easy. They were most grateful and friendly, offering us some of their most recent harvest.

Although I could not stay, I know that our visit to the jungle made an impact. I ask the reader to agree with me in prayer for the conversion and healing of that entire commune. I returned from Hawaii with a keen memory of that particular experience. But before I left the Islands, I made a point of throwing my lei into the ocean.

Back in California I noticed more than ever the announcement in churches and Full Gospel Businessmen's chapters that "Father" Michael Gaydos was coming to speak. It seems the more I protest that title, the less anyone hears. In the Roman Catholic Church "Father" is a term applied to one who has received full ordination to the priesthood.

For years some of my favorite uncles and aunts had been calling me "Father Mike" as a term of endearment. It stopped temporarily while I was in business school, but resumed again when I announced my intentions to enter seminary. With ordination to minor orders I was now a cleric, but full ordination to the priesthood actually takes place in seven steps over a period of four years. Once I received minor orders I began to wear the cassock when I assisted in services and parish work. Most of the members of these various parishes called me "Father Mike," even though they were aware that I was still a seminarian.

I have never introduced myself as a priest, and of course I am not permitted to give the sacraments. If I can do it without seeming too awkward, I explain that I am merely Michael Gaydos, an ordained cleric, but not fully ordained to the priesthood. If I am introduced as "Father," I normally begin by saying that I am an "expectant father," and the congregation responds with good-natured laughter. Sometimes people will then call me "Brother Mike," but usually for lack of knowing how to title me, both Catholic and Protestant will invariably address me as "Father Michael Gaydos." There has been some misunderstanding on occasion; Protestants in particular will note my age and my years of education and simply assume that I am a fully ordained priest. But I have long since given up the tedious and easily misunderstood explanations. I tell them simply that I am a cleric ordained to minor orders on leave of absence, then merely let people call me what they will. Any name would be better than some of the nicknames I endured as a boy.

I am on the Planning Committee for the Greater Pittsburgh Charismatic Conference. Each year I look forward to this event with great anticipation. Shortly after the trip to Hawaii I made my way back home to Pittsburgh for the May 1972 Conference.

I had also been invited to attend a Catholic Pentecostal

conference held in May at Carlow College in Pittsburgh. At the College the wife of a professor from West Virginia University was present. God has apparently healed Dr. Traynelis of cancer that had spread throughout his body. Although he had been told he had only six months to live in February 1971, today Dr. Traynelis is obviously healthier than he has been for many years.

The Traynelises are devout Roman Catholics. When they received the dismal prognosis, both felt at peace. They availed themselves of the Church's ministries. A prayer group met at their home and prayed for his healing. All recent tests have been negative.

But Elaine Traynelis had problems of her own. Ever since they had made their home in Morgantown, she had been afflicted with a peculiar eye condition. The thin covering over the eye would break open without warning.

"This might occur in either eye at any moment," Elaine told me. "I never knew when it was going to happen, and it was always painful when it occurred. The doctor could not explain the condition. The usual treatment was to bandage the afflicted eye tightly until it healed. I could not drive or fulfill my duties as wife, mother, and teacher whenever it happened. If I moved the unbandaged eye, the pain in the damaged eye was almost unbearable. I would simply have to lie flat on my back for at least two days before the condition would disappear again. Then the attacks began coming oftener, and I lived in constant fear of them. They also were lasting longer—up to five days.

"At the conference at Carlow College you were pointed out to me, Mike, as a young man with the gift of healing eyes. I saw you periodically through the day, but hesitated to approach you. At the closing mass I was filled by the Lord with such love and faith that I wondered if God were not prompting me to ask you to intercede for me. I stepped out on faith: 'Lord, we are *not* going to move away from Morgantown because of my eyes! I know you can remove this problem.' So I asked you to pray for me, Mike.

"You placed your hands on the sides of my head and then you prayed first in English and followed with prayer in tongues.

"A shock went through my body, and was gone just as quickly as I felt it. I knew in every cell of my body that I was healed. As I walked up the aisle, a woman seized my arm and exclaimed, 'Oh, something wonderful has just happened here!'

"I returned home with confidence. In the following days I noticed that some of the same irritants, such as frying bacon, peeling onions, and smoke would make my eyes itch and water. But each time I would quickly assert my faith in Jesus Christ and His healing power. The condition would disappear. Today, six months later, I can attest to that miracle. My eyes have never since needed to be bandaged. Praise God! We just don't have words in human language to express my feelings of joy!"

10

God Enlarges My Family

A few months before, I had spoken in Escondido, California. As I had given my testimony, one of those who displayed their faith by removing their glasses was Mrs. Paul Schmid, a Roman Catholic wife and mother then living in Oceanside. Immediately her eyes began to get better. Today she can read all but the finest print and can even thread a needle without glasses. And her eyesight continues to improve. That day in Escondido Mary Schmid not only removed her glasses, she threw them away. There seems to be a very fine line between faith and presumption. Hers was an act of faith.

So many of the homes to which I am invited have already experienced one or more eye healings through my ministry. My visit then becomes a continuing opportunity to praise the Lord for His power and His goodness. I anticipated such a visit at the Schmid home, but I hardly expected to receive so many delightful bonuses.

Paul Schmid is a real estate developer. The family

moved to California from Iowa in 1965 after their two oldest children were married. The Schmids eagerly shared their testimonies with me as I enjoyed their hospitality for that week in August.

Mary Schmid is a precious Christian. She has always been the kind of a Christian I could understand. Solidly Roman Catholic and possessing a deep love for the Lord, she has all her life tried daily to live for Him. "Our lives were drastically changed in 1965 when we moved to California with our six youngest sons," Mary told me. "As I look back now, I realize that we were rather complacent, even to the point of being proud of the fact that we were 'good' Catholics. We kept the commandments of God and the commandments of the Church. God has given me strong maternal instincts, so our large family of seven boys and one girl was a joy and not a burden. We enrolled all six boys in Catholic school, the oldest three in Mater Dei High School in Santa Ana. Paul and I counted heavily upon the teaching and guidance of the priests and nuns, as we had back in Iowa.

"But life was different here in California, and it was changing rapidly. I felt as if I had been transferred to another planet, where evil reigned. A sense of helplessness began to overtake me as I tried to cope with the problems of raising a family in such a world. Back in Iowa 'good' had been a decent word. In the news and entertainment media we seemed surrounded by senseless killings, ugly and distorted hate-filled faces, marijuana and other drugs, hippies and cycle gangs, race riots, and just plain hate. 'Do your own thing!' seemed to be on everyone's lips. Is this how twentieth-century people 'did their own thing?'

"I had been wondering about our own children. When I heard the gospel read from the pulpit, it said that as a boy 'Jesus kept increasing in wisdom and stature, and in favor with God and men.' When our children were small they dearly loved God and the Blessed Mother. But as they grew older, instead of growing closer to God they drifted further from Him. This bothered me increasingly for many years. Was it my fault? Should I blame it on society in general?

"Then tragedy struck our family. Eric, a junior at Mater Dei High School, was expelled for possession of marijuana. The nightmare in our personal lives had begun!"

Mary Schmid spent the next few days going to every high school in the community, pleading with them to enroll Eric. After some weeks he was accepted at Valley High School. Paul and Mary thought that moving Eric to an environment away from his "friends" might give him a new start on dealing with his problems. Within a brief period, court, probation, police all became part of the Schmid family life. Several of the other boys began experimenting with drugs also.

"I couldn't understand what was happening to our family," Mary agonized. "Our home was filled with ugliness—tension, harsh words, intolerably loud music (or was it merely noise?), profanity, fighting among brothers. We even began to experience fear whenever the telephone rang. Every telephone conversation was spoken in hushed tones so the rest of the family could not hear. The boys would come home from school with cigarette burns on their clothing. Many of their possessions were stolen at school and the boys didn't even seem to care. I was praying desperately for God to do something."

Eric was a sensitive young man. During his teen years he began to take a hard look at the world about him. The adult world looked phony and materialistic. The government was wrong for being in Vietnam. The police were prejudiced and power-hungry. The world appeared selfish, hate-filled, and ugly. He wanted no part of it.

As Eric told me, "I set out looking for a freedom—a freedom filled with love and peace and truth and happiness. I became dissatisfied with the mechanical life of the Church. We all received the sacraments of the Roman

Catholic Church, we attended mass every Sunday, prayed before meals, sometimes said the Rosary together, and went to Confession the last Saturday of each month. But our prayers were stereotyped, our confessions were always of the same sins, and we went to early mass in order to get our obligation over with so we could have the rest of the day for ourselves. We were—except for our mother— only obeying the rules. We knew the letter of the law, but not the spirit. On the outside we were good Catholics, but on the inside the spiritual man was dead.

"When I was fifteen years old, a freshman at Mater Dei High School, I started getting 'high' on marijuana. Soon I was making 'connections' and dealing the drug myself. This only led me deeper into drugs, and I began taking amphetamines and barbiturates. Becoming more carefree with the drugs, I would get 'stoned' before and after school, before going to bed, whenever I was with my buddies, and simply every chance I had. Then, as a junior, I 'got busted' for possession of marijuana and a felony established my police record.

"My parents were shocked and horrified to learn that one of their sons was on drugs. Our Catholic school administrators were disappointed to discover that one of their students had been using drugs. After transferring to the public school, I found an ample supply in this school where at least 60 percent of the students were using drugs.

"Along with all my dissatisfaction about the whole world, I could sense that my own life was empty and without purpose. I knew there was more to life than anything I had seen or experienced. Then as I listened to myself, I heard my heart cry out for God. Immediately I knew that the freedom I wanted, that freedom filled with love and peace and truth and happiness, would only come from God.

"I was so disillusioned with the mechanical nature of my childhood Roman Catholicism. I began searching. I was already practicing mediation under Maharishi Mahesh

Yogi. But after two years of this I still had that same emptiness and longing inside, so I tried mediating under Pa-
ramahansa Yogananda. Then to Maher Baba and into
reading Kahlil Gibran's books and then into reading and
studying the Urancia Book.

"In December 1969, my friend Sam and I decided to
spend a few days up in the Big Bear Mountains to 'find
ourselves' through meditation. One day I was sitting alone,
meditating under a tree. As my mind wandered, I pondered the idea of Jesus Christ being the Son of God, instead of merely a great man or a prophet. The desperate
emptiness and hunger within me urged me to cry out,
'Jesus, if You are really the Son of God, then You can
hear me!' I continued my very logical appeal, 'Jesus, if
You are actually alive today, show me, and I'll believe on
You!'

"Suddenly the power of God touched me. I began to
feel quite elated and light-headed. In that instant I knew
that Jesus *is* the Son of God. I knew He was with me. He
filled me with an overflowing joy. Within a few brief
moments all I could do was laugh for joy in the wonderful
presence of Jesus.

"Then I realized another quick truth. I had never
really looked to Jesus before. I became sharply aware that
I was full of sin and selfishness. I cried to Jesus and told
Him I was sorry. I laughed and I cried. I laughed and
cried for about an hour. All the burdens I'd been carrying
for years were suddenly lifted. Jesus answered all my questions about the meaning of life, love, and truth even before I could ask Him.

"Then came the most soothing, comforting, and healing
peace. Jesus knew that my mind needed this healing. For
several weeks that peace continued to flow into every
part of my messed-up mind and life. Taking drugs for five
years had given me a poor memory; I was paranoid, self-
conscious, self-degrading, fearful, mistrusting, and confused. These are more than just words to me. They were

very real, painful, and sorrowful experiences from which I had slowly begun to suspect there was no escape.

"But Jesus loved me. He waited until the time was right, until I was ready. Then He drew me to Himself. I had walked every path I ever heard of to try to find God. But Jesus said, 'No one can come to Me, unless the Father who sent Me draws him.' And it's true!

"The change that took place within me affected every part of my life and everything that touched my life, including my friends. I could not resist telling them about Jesus. I had something so good and so real I had to share it."

Eric's mother interposed, "I looked at Eric when he returned home from the mountains. His countenance was radiant. His whole being was aglow with warmth and enthusiasm. There was something of Christ in Eric that could be seen visibly. I turned away and cried silently— for joy!

"Eric's life immediately was filled with peace and joy. He was so helpful and so considerate! Then he became involved with the 'Jesus People' of Calvary Chapel in Costa Mesa and The King's Hacienda in San Clemente. Eric asked all of us to attend services there with him. As he related tales of miraculous healings, receiving the Holy Spirit, speaking in tongues, changed lives—I wanted to go. I watched some of Eric's friends change as he had after they attended those services. Their experiences were often as dramatic and beautiful as Eric's had been."

One day Mary suggested to Paul that they all go to Calvary Chapel or The King's Hacienda to see these things for themselves. "I may as well have suggested a trip to hell," Mary laughed.

Paul was shocked. "Already Eric isn't going to mass with us on Sunday, and you want to confuse and undermine our younger children by going to another church! Just forget it!—unless by chance you have the Pope's approval. We will never go to that church, nor will we allow the other boys to go!"

Mary continued: "One week later Paul came to me alone and said he'd take me to King's Hacienda if I still wanted to go. His intention was to demonstrate to me how it really was—money-grabbing, false doctrine, etc.—and that would end it once and for all.

"What he saw was hundreds of glowing faces, genuine joy, and singing so beautiful that it seemed celestial. Yet it was all spontaneous, never practiced. These people were intent only upon worshiping God—often with their arms outstretched—and obviously with all their hearts. We couldn't find what was wrong, so Paul said we'd go back again. This time we would discover what was crooked about that church. We returned again and again—never able to find the error. Everything was interdenominational. Nobody said a thing to undermine my Roman Catholic faith.

"We began attending Calvary Chapel—dumbfounded to discover that if we wanted a seat we had to come two hours early. In every service we watched people accepting Jesus, receiving the Holy Spirit with the speaking in tongues, and being healed in their bodies. We watched kids, upon being filled with the Holy Spirit, give up every form of drugs, including heroin. They betrayed no withdrawal effects, and instead became 'high' on the 'new wine!' We were astonished to behold the fantastic changes in these kids. It was hard to believe they had ever lost their childhood innocence.

"I have known Jesus personally since childhood, yet there was more here. We were being drawn irresistibly toward a total commitment to Jesus Christ."

Paul was the most stubborn of the Schmids. He had a way of life which he never questioned. He worked hard and expected his boys to work hard too. The family also operated a large motel, and the work was always there to be done. Paul still refused to accept all this "new" stuff.

Then Maria found Jesus. Maria was Paul's secretary in his real estate office. She was so tired and so bored with work that she spent her evenings drinking. Eric and his friends introduced Maria to Jesus, and all night long she cried out her sin and sorrow. Jesus made Maria a new creation. In spite of her lack of sleep, Maria went to work with a twinkle in her eyes and a smile from ear to ear. Week after week Paul felt the growing conviction of seeing radiantly changed lives. Finally the pressure caused him to make that first trip to The King's Hacienda.

"I was so impressed by the way those young people sang," Paul said. "I had never seen such freedom in singing. And their *eyes*—so clear and bright and full of love and joy! How often the name of Jesus was mentioned! Their worship was so sincere. But I didn't want to admit at the time that I had been impressed."

Mary Schmid went on as I eagerly listened to the unfolding of the Schmid family drama. "Soon our day came. At one service when the question was asked, 'Who wants to give his life to the Lord?' Paul and I and Kevin and John made that commitment."

Eric laughed about sixteen-year-old Greg. "He wasn't so sure about all this. But I gently kept after him and finally he too gave his life to Jesus."

Greg had an interesting experience with his marijuana. He wasn't convinced there was anything wrong with smoking marijuana, so he walked out on the beach one day after he had invited Jesus to take over his life. Greg was about half-way through his first cigarette when he began wondering why he wasn't getting "high." The marijuana no longer had any effect on him! Suddenly the Holy Spirit hit Greg with such conviction in his heart that he tore apart the remaining cigarettes and threw them away!

That week in August was a glorious time of sharing with a family where the entire household is committed to Jesus. Paul and Mary led their boys in Bible study, prayer, and singing. We often sang together in the Spirit. The Schmids as a family are waiting upon the Lord for direction for their lives.

Mary commented on how God is continuing to heal her eyes; she can now read all but the finest of print. Then she summed up her experience: "I love the mass. In it is enacted the Last Supper and Jesus' giving His life for us. It's the greatest love story ever told. Through the 'Jesus People' we have been drawn so much closer to the Lord. People often comment on how our boys 'never seem to fight with each other.' We are no longer dedicated to 'doing our own thing.' We are completely dedicated to 'doing God's thing.' Sometimes my innermost being cries out, 'It would take an eternity to express my gratitude for what the Lord has done in our lives!' "

It was such a joy to spend time in the Schmid home! Many precious homes on the West Coast have been opened to me, and I have enjoyed them all. There is one special family in Visalia, California. Stephen and Linda Souza have both made such an impact upon me. When I first spoke in their community, I prayed for Stephen to be baptized in the Holy Spirit. Immediately I was almost a member of their family.

Stephen's priorities changed strikingly. In a job where worldly pressures abound, he now witnesses for the Lord. Stephen's sales manager is concerned that his top salesman-evangelist is going to lose sales if he doesn't "cut out this Christian stuff." He and Linda took a teenage Catholic girl—a ward of the Welfare Department—into their home. Cecile quickly began to question whether the Souzas were indeed Roman Catholic, as the authorities had promised her, for she had never heard Catholics going around the house praising the Lord. Her suspicions were not allayed until Sunday, when to Cecile's relief they took her to Holy Family Catholic Church. Since then Cecile has accepted the Lord and been baptized in the Holy Spirit, completely transformed from a frightened, rejected, rebellious youngster into a pleasant addition to the Souza family.

Linda Souza is to me a good example of how a Spirit-filled Christian mother can serve the Lord—in interests apart from the immediate family—and yet not deprive the family of her needed presence as homemaker. In addition to having Cecile as a foster daughter, Linda now is an emergency counselor for girls considering abortion. She has a "hot line" right into her home. Stephen and Linda both seem to approach God with that childlike simplicity Jesus described. They are joyful and filled with anticipation·of an exciting future with Him. Again I rejoice in being able to minister to a family and watch such dramatic results.

In late summer of 1972 I left the Souza home again to speak in northern California and in the Northwest. I enjoyed a return visit to Springs of Living Water. While I was there a nearly blind monk in his seventies was brought to the Springs. Brother Bob is from the Trappist Monastery, one of the strictest orders in the Catholic Church. The Abbot of New Clairvaux Abbey drove him to the meeting. On the way home Brother Bob could see clearly, and he once again began to drive a car.

This humble Trappist monk is an example for those who have no faith for healing of their eyes "because I'm too old." I know that God intends His children to live victoriously all the years of our earthly lives. If "Moses was one hundred and twenty years old when he died" and "his eye was not dim," then we who love the same God can expect the same undimmed physical vision as well. No need to accept the limitations placed upon us by an unbelieving world! I just received a letter from a ninety-year-old woman requesting prayer for her eyes. That letter thrills me.

I traveled to Arcata, California, after my stay at Springs of Living Water. One week before my arrival, the pastor of the First Baptist Church announced that I was coming and that I had a special ministry for eyes. Darlene Steele is a member of First Baptist Church of Arcata. As she told me later, Darlene knew instantly that God would heal her eyes on the following Sunday. She worked all week with the joy of anticipation in her heart.

That was a Baptist service to talk about. I tried to end the service a little after the traditional hour of twelve noon, but the congregation would have none of it. Finally at 2:30 we concluded one of the most striking Sunday worship services I have ever seen. I then prayed for Darlene, and the Lord healed her eyes instantly.

I spoke at the Methodist Church that evening. During the service the Holy Spirit urged me to "pray for ears." Darlene testified to "a quick, instant movement" in her ears as God healed her partial loss of hearing, a handicap she had long since accepted fatalistically.

A number of people in Arcata testified that "we'll never be the same after this day!" I could easily have added, "Nor will I!"

I continued on to speaking engagements in Oregon and Washington. I was scheduled to be in Tacoma for several days, beginning on a Wednesday evening. The pastor announced my coming on the previous Sunday morning, and during that Sunday service he called for a congregational rededication to Jesus Christ.

A young man named Paul Morehouse eagerly responded to that invitation. A few minutes later the power of God surged through his body, and Paul felt a very strong urging to remove his glasses. Paul had only recently accepted Jesus Christ. He had been on drugs for several years, even to the point of being a "junkie" while serving in the Army in Vietnam. He was "young" in the Lord.

But Paul resisted the urge. Again, an even stronger surge of power went through him, and the Spirit's message was more insistent than before: "Take off your glasses!"

He took them off and grabbed his Bible. Excitedly Paul read Scripture which had been illegible without glasses for years. Indeed, he never could read so well, even as a child. He looked to the front of the church to see clearly everything that would have appeared hazy just ten minutes before. As the service ended, Paul rushed to the front in tears and fell to his knees in worship.

When Paul told his pastor what had happened, the pastor began to prophesy: "This is just the beginning!" said the Lord in the words of prophecy. Others gathered around to share Paul's joy and tears.

On my second evening in that church—Thursday—the power of God fell upon the congregation. Many received eye healings within a few minutes. Among them was Connie, Paul's lovely wife.

"I could just feel the presence of God while you were speaking!" Connie exclaimed. "Suddenly God touched my eyes and I knew He was healing them." Connie walked to the front and placed her glasses on the altar.

"I had worn glasses since I was seven years old because of nearsightedness and double vision. Without glasses I would have headaches, my eyes would cross, and of course I could hardly see. Today—after only one week—I can see normally, both at a distance and up close. I praise God for all He's done!"

Now with normal physical vision, Paul and Connie are eagerly serving the Lord, for their spiritual vision has increased comparably.

In the midst of the flow of eye-healings, God is always healing other ailments too. I am excited about everything the Lord does. For example, I received a letter from Corona, California, sometime after I had spoken there. The letter spoke of a girl with whom I had prayed following the service. In addition to her eyes, she was suffering from a serious condition that affected her kidneys. She was scheduled to enter the hospital for surgery the next day. That night she developed a sudden cold and the surgery was postponed. By the time the infection cleared up, so had the kidneys. Her doctors were actually embarrassed at being unable to find anything wrong. Praise the Lord! And she reported that her eyes were improving too. Additional letters continue to testify to other such healings.

I am always most thrilled of all when folks accept the Lord: that is the most meaningful of all. A suspicious Protestant woman from Portland, Oregon, heard me speak recently. Something wonderful happened in her heart that day as the Holy Spirit introduced her to Jesus. Carol wrote to tell me that for several nights in a row the Spirit woke her out of her usually very sound sleep. Five or six times each night she awoke suddenly to sense a warm, protected feeling, other times to hear a voice say, "I love you." Other delightful miracles and changes began occurring in her life, including deliverance from cigarettes.

Carol concluded, "I felt I had to write and tell you of the difference in my life since I heard you speak August 26."

These are the stories that excite me most. Each one means that another soul has received eternal life, and that's really what it's all about.

11

The Holy Spirit Uses Electronics

At first the little black box called a cassette recorder seemed like a mild threat whenever I was speaking. Gradually I became accustomed to its presence and rather ignored it. In recent months however, the recorder's value has been shown so clearly that I can now rejoice when I see them being carried into the services.

I had received a very occasional testimony of a healing that took place as someone listened to a tape of one of my meetings, so its worth seemed quite marginal to my ministry. But after two years of witnessing to God's grace, the "tape testimonies" are increasing. The anointing of the Holy Spirit goes wherever the tape goes!

As an example, here is the testimony of one taped service as God placed it in the hands of a lovely Spirit-filled couple in Pittsburgh. Steve and Dorothy Totin are Byzantine Catholics. A friend had given the Totins some cassette tapes as a gift. Recorded on one of the tapes was a service in which I had spoken. Dorothy played that tape for Joan one dramatic afternoon.

Joan's arms and hands were almost useless and her body was wracked with pain. In April 1972 Joan mustered her courage and went to see a doctor. Instead of the brain tumor she expected, the doctor found arthritis of the spine, diabetes, and a breast tumor. Joan was depressed and fearful. The tumor was removed immediately. Later the doctor discovered a second tumor of the breast, and another operation was performed in June.

While her doctors were considering surgery on the spine, Joan attended a wedding where she met Steve and Dorothy. Steve told Joan what God could do for her; then they prayed for her. Joan was cautious and noncommittal. While Steve and Dorothy continued to pray for Joan, the gift tapes were received, and Joan finally agreed to listen. Because Joan was Roman Catholic, Dorothy selected my tape and played it for her. Joan arrived depressed and filled with pain; she left the house free!

Several weeks later her neurosurgeon was saying again and again, "Someone must have been praying! Someone must have been praying awfully hard!" All symptoms of sickness were completely gone, and the surgeon was very much aware of the One who did it. Another examination revealed no trace of diabetes.

Dolores was another acquaintance whose mind was in a terrible condition. Dolores had sought help from various Catholic priests to no avail. She then turned to Protestant ministers in a desperate effort to be freed from an unbearable emotional state. Dolores' turmoil only increased. She began weekly therapy with a psychiatrist. Nothing improved. Dolores is quite intelligent and by nature religious. She stormed against this "unfeeling, unresponsive" God; she fought with her neighbors, her family, her Church.

Several months ago Dolores collapsed on what she describes as her "one and only source of comfort of the past miserable years"—her sofa—and said simply to God, "If I have been tempting you, I'm truly sorry. You'll just have to show me."

Within hours she met Dorothy Totin. Since Dorothy seemed so sympathetic, Dolores told of her problems. Some days later Dorothy phoned to ask if she could bring a tape and play it for her. Dolores listened suspiciously to what I was saying, waiting to find my "gimmick."

At the end of the taped service a hymn was sung. Dorothy and Dolores stood and held hands. Suddenly the top of Dolores' head was enveloped in "pure heat." Within several days she received glorious deliverance. "I am amazed at the swiftness with which the Lord worked," Dolores said recently. "My sorrow is gone and I have found a Friend. Praise God, I'm back in my own Church again!"

Steve and Dorothy's tape really traveled! Every time it was played, the Totins would be praying earnestly. Ida Mae listened to the tape one day, and she and Dorothy prayed for Ida Mae's young daughter, who had been severely burned. At the close of the taped service, I had asked everyone to hold hands and pray with me. Dorothy, Ida Mae, and another friend present in the home held hands and prayed for little Diane as that final part of the taped service wound through the recorder. Again the Holy Spirit fell upon the group of listeners, even as He had fallen upon the large congregation several months before.

Ida Mae and her friends had begun to pray as soon as the fire had occurred. In the hospital the doctor said that 60 percent of Diane's body—her entire right side—had been burned. She was transferred to another hospital with a special burn unit. By now only 23 percent of her skin was burned. Ida Mae continued to request prayer. In response, Dorothy Totin asked her to listen to the tape of my service. Ida Mae *knew* something was happening to Diane at the moment the taped service concluded.

The day after hearing the tape, the surgeon told the mother that Diane would require extensive operations to graft skin on her arm, hand, leg, and foot.

"No, Doctor," Ida Mae replied. "I believe now that God is healing her body. She won't need that surgery."

Within a day or so the plans were changed. Only the leg and foot would need surgery now. Ida Mae rejoiced to witness the Lord's healing, but she was tormented by little Diane's constant pain.

Finally the surgeon told the mother that even the leg and foot would heal without surgery, but it would require about a year. Ida Mae thought of her daughter's intense suffering and consented to the surgery. The doctor envisioned the need for several pints of blood and two or three other operations to follow. No blood was needed during surgery and the remaining skin healed without another operation. The transplanted area was quite small. Diane was hospitalized only ten weeks—long enough to witness the repeated tragedy of the other burned children brought into the unit. Of all the children who had been burned as badly as Diane, not one survived. What a difference Jesus can make—even from tragedy to glory!

As I was preparing to leave for my second overseas trip, I stopped at a hospital to visit a friend. While I was there, the thought occurred to me that I might get the required cholera shot at the hospital. I went to the emergency room and inquired.

"Certainly," the nurse responded. "Just have a seat and we'll call you."

A teenage girl was screaming with pain. I sat down only to have a feeling of conviction come over me. So I asked the nurse if she minded my praying for the girl. Then I walked over to her mother and asked if I could pray with her pain-wracked daughter. She consented. I prayed briefly, then softly sang "Alleluia." The girl relaxed and became quiet.

I sat down again. A black woman brought her crying

five-year-old into the emergency room. Again the conviction in my spirit. I got up and asked his mother the
same question. Then I prayed with the boy and sang
quietly—all this in the hectic atmosphere of a hospital
emergency room—"Jesus Loves Me." He too became settled and the emergency room was relatively quiet.

Just then the nurse called, "All right, Father, we're
ready for you now."

After I received the shot I reached for my money. "How
much do I owe you?"

The nurse smiled broadly. "Oh, Father. This one's on
the house. Have a good trip and God bless you!"

I also took care of a matter I had dreaded. My left eye
still has not received that final healing touch. I know that
Jesus accomplished my healing on the cross, and I know
that its physical manifestation will be complete. I made
an appointment with the optometrist who has my records
for some years in the past.

After all, I had been counseling people who had been
healed to get their driver's licenses changed. Now I was
back home and occasionally driving my father's car—
without glasses, but with the "Corrective lenses required"
still on my license.

The optometrist was astonished to note that my right
eye was 20:20. However, the left eye still lacked central
vision. "There's nothing that glasses can do for you," he
said, and promptly filled out the necessary form to revise
my driver's license. That confirmed the complete healing
of my one eye and the partial healing of the other. And I
know that the whole package is mine. My Father wants
me whole.

The Rector of Holy Apostles Seminary often told me
that I was "naive." What he meant was that I have a childlike and simplistic view of God, the Church, people, and
life. To this day some of my best friends make similar
observations about me. Such comments might bother me
had Jesus not said so emphatically, "Truly I say to you,

unless you are converted and become like children, you shall not enter the kingdom of heaven. Whoever then humbles himself as this child, he is the greatest in the kingdom of heaven." (Matthew 18:3,4) My story may seem childlike, but I have discovered that God honors childlike Christians.

The raising of hands in worship is a good example. Many Christians seem too sophisticated, too proud, to raise their hands in praise of the Lord who died for them. The psalmist repeatedly urges us to raise our hands in worship. St. Paul ordains it: "I want the men in every place to pray, lifting up holy hands, without wrath and dissension." (1 Timothy 2:8) When we allow our pride to be crucified, God accepts us. The raising of our hands in sincere worship, unafraid of the judgments of other people, accomplishes great things within our hearts.

This gesture reminds me so much of Jesus, hanging on the cross with His arms outstretched and saying, "I love you. I love you so much that I have died that your sins might be forgiven and that you might have life." The raising of hands reminds me of saying, "I surrender, Lord. You are the Lord of my life. I want Your will to be accomplished in my life rather than my own will." It reminds me too of saying with the psalmist, "Bless the Lord, O my soul; and all that is within me, bless His Holy Name!" It further reminds me of saying, "Lord, I want more. I want more of you." It reminds me also of a boy riding a bicycle with his hands in the air: "Look Mom! No hands! I'm free!—free from bondage and guilt and fear!"

A few months ago I was invited to speak at the first anniversary celebration of the charismatic prayer group at Immaculate Conception Roman Catholic Church in Washington, Pennsylvania. Exactly one year before I had been invited to speak to a large number in the congregation about the Charismatic Renewal. At the end of that earlier service I felt directed by the Holy Spirit to do something different.

"Anybody here who does *not* wish to receive Jesus Christ as Lord or anybody who does *not* wish to be baptized in the Holy Spirit, please raise your hand."

No hands were raised. There was only a sea of expectant, eager faces in front of me. So I prayed for salvation in Jesus Christ and I prayed that they all be filled with the Holy Spirit.

The power of God fell upon that church. Joy began to flow. Many began to speak in tongues. And a local Pentecostal pastor seated at the rear almost swallowed his teeth. He could hardly believe what he was seeing.

We had a delightful anniversary celebration together.

I am so excited about everything the Holy Spirit is doing in the Roman Catholic Church all across the world. Pope John, when he began Vatican Council II, prayed a prophetic prayer for a new Pentecost in the Church. What I have experienced these past two years is an answer to Pope John's prayer. Many other Catholics have also prayed that we might see God's Spirit poured out and the prophecy of Joel 2:28,29 fulfilled. I was so filled with joy to visit Notre Dame University in June of 1972 to see 12,000 Christians—mostly Catholics—assembled together under one roof, lifting their hands in praise to the Lord, recognizing that Jesus is Lord of His people, each one singing in a different tongue, witnessing the demonstration of the Spirit's power and seeing the manifestation of His fruits— that is, His character—in our lives.

While visiting in the Chicago area I was pleased to visit the Catholic Pentecostal community in Geneva, incorporated by the Diocese of Rockford as a charismatic congregation. There several hundred Roman Catholics celebrate the liturgy and worship by singing in the Spirit. Miraculous signs and wonders follow.

In New Orleans I rejoiced to celebrate the Eucharist with five Spirit-filled priests and a Catholic congregation of 500 worshiping in the power of the Holy Spirit.

The Pittsburgh community of Catholic Pentecostals is a

dynamic fellowship. They emphasize strongly a continuing study of the Bible and training for the Spirit-filled life. As a result, hundreds of Catholic Pentecostals in the Pittsburgh area are solid, serving Christians, eagerly evangelistic, and quite effective. Every congregation in the Pittsburgh Diocese, I am certain, has been touched by the Charismatic Renewal. It is so wonderful to see old friends with a new glow.

But to this day my parents don't know quite what to think about their unorthodox son. My mother often needles me about being a "holy roller." Although I am much more faithful to the Church than my parents, yet somehow they feel I'm not "Catholic" enough. By now the give-and-take has become the household joke.

Recently Uncle John, my Confirmation sponsor, died. I was privileged to participate in the funeral liturgy. As we were preparing to leave home, my mother exclaimed, "Michael, you *are* wearing your black suit, aren't you?"

I smiled.

A few minutes later we were ready to go, and she spoke firmly, "For goodness' sake, Michael, when we get to the funeral home, *act Catholic!*"

I nearly choked with laughter. What can I say?

The funeral liturgy was so inspiring. Formerly we had a black pall over the casket, the priest wore black vestments, and the music was mournful and depressing. Today the liturgical renewal has gloriously revised this to make it more distinctly Christian. The pall is white and the vestments are white—to emphasize the resurrection. The paschal candle is lighted. The liturgy called for me to read that very appropriate Scripture from Romans 6:5. The priest's eloquent and comforting homily obviously came from a true pastor's heart. The entire service pointed to the resurrection of Jesus Christ and our share in it. I had talked and prayed with my Uncle John during his illness, and it grieved us all to lose him, but we were greatly encouraged by the words of the new liturgy. Yet I note with sadness that the liturgical changes are not appreciated by all Catholics. They're not—or at least they don't seem—well, "Catholic" enough.

On Thanksgiving Day 1972 I was at home, preparing a slide presentation to show my family some pictures of all the places I had been during the previous year. I was heavy-hearted as I put together the exciting record, for I sensed my family would rather watch television. My sister-in-law, Mary Margaret, who is affectionately known in our family by the nickname "Butch," walked into my room where I was kneeling on the floor, putting slides in order.

"How are you doing, Michael?"

"Okay."

"Are you sure you're okay?" Butch persisted.

"Yes, Butch. I'm okay." My lowered eyes were filling.

She gently placed her hand on my shoulder and knelt beside me. Butch began to pray quietly, and within that remarkable prayer she detailed every concern on my heart. The Holy Spirit told her exactly how to pray!

"Butch!" I thought. "Oh, Butch! You understand! Oh, Jesus! You've done something for Butch! She's a new creation! You've heard my prayers! Oh, thank you, Jesus!" And then I really cried.

As I tell my story I am grateful for my *past*—for my history, my culture, my Church, my schools, my family, my experiences. In spite of all the pain involved I am grateful for the shortcomings, the failures, the rejections, the hunger, the need. I am in awe of the *present*—to see what God is doing in my heart and in my life daily as I walk where He leads by His Spirit and as I continue to grow in Christ. And I am in tremendous anticipation of the *future*. Not only my own future, in which I watch the Lord unfolding His plan for my life, but also the future of the entire Church—all the people of God as He continues to manifest His signs and wonders in our midst.

I do not mean to say that I am somehow "better" or "more useful" in the Kingdom of God than anyone who has not received the baptism in the Holy Spirit. But I do mean to say this—that I am a lot better and a lot more useful in the Kingdom of God than I was three years ago.

And the growth continues. "Please be patient. God is not finished with me yet." So reads a button some Christians are wearing these days. That's one of the qualities the baptism in the Holy Spirit provides—a willingness to grow in the Lord—and keep on growing.

For example, I was eating a light breakfast in a restaurant some time ago. The bill was one dollar. I left the waitress a quarter tip. As I walked away from the table, the Lord spoke to me. "Why did you leave the waitress a quarter?"

"Well, Lord, I thought fifteen cents would appear cheap. After all, I'm wearing this collar."

"Do you mean that you'd rather appear cheap to Me than to this waitress?"

"What do you mean, Lord?"

"You will give her twenty-five percent to avoid appearing cheap, but you won't give Me even My *ten* percent."

I was never trained to tithe. Actually, I seldom made much money, and in my teaching jobs I had saved money which I later spent on my seminary education. But now I had been out speaking for a full year, and normally I receive an honorarium when I give my witness. I began to squirm.

"Well, I'm in the Lord's work," I reasoned. So I asked a clergyman if I could invest my tithe in my own ministry. He smiled, but he wouldn't give me the answer I wanted. So now I'm a tither, and I've already discovered its rewards. As I said, "I want to keep on growing."

Meanwhile He keeps on working. Several weeks ago I spoke in Pastor Wallace Faas' South Greensburg, Pennsylvania, United Methodist Church. A few days later a very dear friend, the Reverend David Curry, met me at our Interfaith Ministers' Fellowship luncheon.

"Mike, I was at the Jesus Barn last Thursday. Two young people stood up and testified of how God had healed their eyes in the South Greensburg Methodist Church," David said.

A few weeks later a friend of mine received a letter written by a young man who was present at that service. He showed me the letter. I was so impressed that this young college student had grasped an understanding of what faith is. In fact, I could not improve on parts of his letter.

"I was home for Thanksgiving vacation. We got to church a little early; I said hello to a few high school friends. During the service Father Mike spoke on faith," he wrote.

"I had been healed by the Lord of a neck injury three months before so little faith was required. All I had to do was claim the healing. But now the Lord was to begin teaching me what real trust in Him was all about. Father Mike said during his sermon that some in the congregation were being healed at that very moment.

"Instantly I felt a warm glow within me starting from my head and going down to my feet. My heart began pounding. I had the same feeling when the Lord healed my neck. He was telling me to take off my glasses, step out in faith, walk to the front of the sanctuary, and be healed. I was hesitant because of my friends sitting there. I was afraid of what they might think of me. But I knew these thoughts were from 'the chief of the sons of pride'— Satan. I asked the Lord to give me strength to step out in faith.

"My mother asked me if I wanted to go up front. Without hesitating I said, 'Let's go!' So I walked to the front in full view of my friends and took off my glasses. All I had to do was *believe* that I was healed. This is where Christ started teaching me about faith. He is teaching me to believe as a child—not to question or doubt Him—just believe. (Mark 11:24) While I wore glasses I depended upon them for my sight; now I depend solely upon Him for my sight and He hasn't let me down.

"The full manifestation of my healing did not come that night, although He did improve them markedly. And He continues to improve them. Also, He wants me to keep thanking and praising Him for healing my eyes. This is the most wonderful Christmas gift I've ever received!"

That young man will receive the rest of his healing.

> Filled with a strange new hope they came—
> The blind, the leper, the sick, the lame—
> Frail of body, spent of soul,
> As many as touched Him were made whole.
> The Christ we follow is still the same,
> With blessings that all who will may claim.
> How often we miss Love's healing touch
> By thinking, "We must not ask too much!"
> —Anon.
> Quoted in Louis O. Caldwell,
> *Miracles of the Master*, Baker, 1970

12

Washing in the Pool of Siloam

"The man who is called Jesus made clay, and anointed my eyes, and said to me, 'Go to Siloam, and wash'; so I went away and washed, and I received sight." (John 9:11)

Scripture tells us that "faith is the assurance of things hoped for, the conviction of things not seen." (Hebrews 11:1)

One of the ways to explain this verse is by a simple illustration. Imagine for a few moments that it is now the first week of December, and you have taken your youngster to see Santa Claus in the department store. First your five-year-old makes an exploration of the entire toy department. He takes note of all the things he wants for Christmas. At the top of his list is a bicycle. He knows the style, the color, the accessories. Then your boy crawls on Santa's lap, and in great detail he tells Santa Claus what he has pictured in his mind's eye—a certain bicycle, with very specific features. As you take the boy's hand to leave the toy department, he now begins to picture in his mind's eye *more* than just the bicycle. He sees himself getting out of bed on Christmas morning, finding the bicycle under the tree, and then riding around the block and showing it off to his friends. He has already thanked Santa for the bicycle. Your son tugs on your hand and confidently announces that he's getting a bike for Christmas.

Why? Because the boy recalls the faithfulness of Santa Claus. He remembers last Christmas with delight, as Santa delivered exactly what he had requested. The youngster does not have faith in the department store, nor in the toy manufacturers. Rather, he has faith in a person—the person of Santa Claus. Your boy actually possesses in his mind's eye the guarantee of the blessings he hopes for, the existence of a bicycle at present unseen. He is convinced that he is getting it before he has the tangible reality in his hands.

So should it be with all of us. We know that God is faithful to His Word, faithful to His promises. Upon accepting and appropriating His Word to our needs, we too can have the evidence of what we ask for in faith. We must have faith in the person of Jesus Christ.

I have been in many services where people have asked me to pray that the Lord will heal their eyes. Frequently I inquire of them, "Do you believe the Lord Jesus Christ will heal your eyes?"

The reply is often, "I think so" or, "Maybe" or, "I hope so."

How wonderful it is to hear, "I believe He will heal me. I really believe it."

When Christians believe the promise of God's Word and are willing to appropriate His Word to answer their needs—in spite of what they might feel at the time I am praying for them—such people are most frequently able to receive their healings. Jesus died on the cross for our salvation; He shed His blood for the forgiveness of our sins; and "with His wounds we were healed."

Our God is a God of variety. Although our healing has

already been accomplished on Calvary, there is a great variety of ways in which we can appropriate that which Jesus gained for us in that atonement. For example, healing may be received when you as a Christian go to another for prayer. You may receive by hearing the preaching of the Word of God and believing what is heard. Healing may be received by proxy, as the centurion, asking for his servant, said to Jesus, "I am not fit for You to come under my roof . . . but say the word, and my servant will be healed." The Lord is not limited by time or space. Your healing may further be received through the anointing with oil by priests, elders, or deacons of the Church. This is called in the Roman Catholic Church the Sacrament of the anointing of the sick. On occasion a Christian will be healed at the time of receiving Communion; if you believe when you participate in the Communion that you are receiving the body and blood of the Lord Jesus Christ —receiving the Lord Himself, receiving the Healer Himself—that point in time could be the very moment when you receive your healing. Many have been healed in services as Christians come together to worship the Lord. The Lord "inhabits the praises" of His people. As we minister to the Lord in worship, He ministers life and wholeness to us.

Do you recall blind Bartimaeus? As recorded in Mark 10, Bartimaeus heard that Jesus of Nazareth was passing by. He shouted, "Jesus, Son of David, have mercy on me!" The crowd tried to restrain Bartimaeus. But the more they tried to hold him back the more he cried out. Perhaps there are people in your life who are trying to hold you back. They may be the people with whom you live, your own family—or the people with whom you work —even those with whom you worship on Sunday. They may be suggesting that you "not go overboard," that you "not become a fanatic about religion."

This sort of restraining pressure from those around did not stop Bartimaeus. And he cried out all the more, "Jesus,

Son of David, have mercy on me!" Bartimaeus knew where the power was; he knew the Source.

Jesus responded to Bartimaeus by asking, "What do you want Me to do for you?"

We are all like Bartimaeus—beggars. Without Jesus we are nothing. He asks us all the same question: "What do you want Me to do for you?"

Jesus did not ask Bartimaeus this question in order to inform Himself. He could see that the beggar was blind. Rather, Jesus was probably asking Bartimaeus to speak with his own lips the words of faith: "Master, let me see again."

James 4:2 says, "You do not have because you do not ask." And to go a step further, we do not pray for what we want because we do not believe. For a long time in my life I was aware of the miraculous—but only aware. I knew the Church accepted miracles. I had heard stories of how people received healing at Fatima or Lourdes, but I had never seen such a healing. I could not very easily catch a plane for one of those places. At least I didn't believe strongly enough to find my way to such a shrine. Frankly, I wasn't praying because I didn't believe.

What a thrilling revelation to me to discover that Jesus is alive right in my own backyard! His signs and wonders can follow anyone who proclaims His gospel. I don't need to travel halfway around the world to experience miracles; miracles follow me, as they will follow any believer who witnesses of Jesus in the power of the Holy Spirit. A Christian is "a miracle finding places to happen." So Jesus is alive and present to *you* as you reach out to receive from Him.

Therefore, *see yourself healed!* As the little boy sees himself riding the bicycle on Christmas Day, so see yourself with 20:20 eyesight. And never lose that vision.

The most remarkable part of this story seems not to be God's healing of my own eyes. Rather, it is that whenever I present my testimony in public meetings and proclaim the Word of God concerning faith and healing, and there are present those who believe and will act upon that Word, the Lord Jesus Christ faithfully heals eyes. This has happened consistently, as you know from reading this book. Several thousand have experienced such healing in their own eyes in two brief years. But healing has occurred also when people have listened to *tapes* of these services. Even in printed form: the message is the same, Jesus is the same.

Perhaps as you have been reading this book, Jesus has been ministering to you. Perhaps you are reaching out in faith. Why not stop for a moment and appropriate—accept—receive—His Word to your need: "Thank you, Lord Jesus, for healing me. I accept this healing right now. I apply Your Word and stand on the authority of that Word. Dear Lord Jesus, thank You for being the Resurrection and the Life. Thank You for imparting Your life to me. May every cell of my body be strengthened and quickened by Your Holy Spirit. In my mind's eye I see myself healed and living normally. Thank You, Lord. Praise Your holy name! Now I have eyes to behold You! Amen."